MY WALK through THE VALLEY

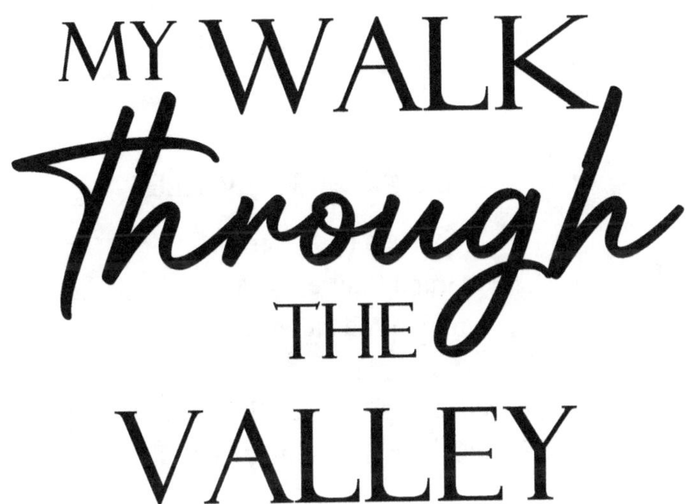

Vempre Terrell, Jr.

V. Terrell
Grand Prairie, Texas

MY WALK *through* THE VALLEY

Published by V. Terrell
Grand Prairie, Texas
vempreterrell@utexas.edu

Vempre Terrell, Jr., Publisher / Editorial Director
Yvonne Rose/Quality Press.info, Book Packager

Copyright © 2024 by Vempre Terrell, Jr.
Print ISBN: 979-8-3304-2111-4
Ebook ISBN: 979-8-3304-2112-1
Library of Congress Control Number: 2024919640

DEDICATION

My Walk Through the Valley is dedicated to every individual who has ever experienced a challenge in life that has called for the need to have faith. Time and time again, it may seem as if giving up is the only option. Even so, never forget that having faith the size of a mustard seed will turn life's tests into powerful testimonies. Always remember that when you have faith, your trust resides in God. When you trust God, all things are possible!

ACKNOWLEDGEMENTS

To begin, I would like to first thank my Heavenly Father for inspiring me to write each word of this book. Whether using motivations from small happenings or life-changing events, God empowered me with a spiritual connection to turn one word into an entire book. Also, it is my pleasure to take the time to thank my family for providing me with everlasting motivation toward my passion for writing.

TABLE OF CONTENTS

MY WALK THROUGH THE VALLEY

With the words of this dynamic book of spiritual motivation, Vempre Terrell, Jr. inspires readers to realize that difficult days of life are not meant to bring about a halt in a downward place, but to inspire a leap into higher places. Many individuals reach obstacles in life that appear to be too much to bear and gravitate toward a natural desire to give up. Nevertheless, Vempre Terrell, Jr. emphasizes that spiritually walking through life's low points is what allows a person to reach better times ahead, not settling at a stopping point. *MY WALK THROUGH THE VALLEY* serves as a spiritual script for grasping faith and releasing fear. By implementing encouraging anecdotes, motivational declarations, and insights from a practical standpoint, Vempre Terrell, Jr. demonstrates how changing one's spiritual view leads to today's trials becoming tomorrow's triumphs.

Chapter One

MY PURPOSE ON THE PATH

What speaks *for* my purpose? What speaks *to* my purpose? What speaks *within* my purpose? What gives life to why I move *toward* my purpose? Questions of this nature tend to flood our minds as we strive to achieve the things that we are pursuing in life. Even so, it is not the questions themselves that are the issues. It is our answers to the questions that are the issues. Taking it a step further, it is our lack of answers to the questions that stand as the issues.

When your phone rings, why do you answer it? When you hear your alarm clock, why do you get out of bed? Both questions have one common answer: *you have a purpose*. I cannot say enough that when you know what your purpose happens to be, life moves much smoother. Answering your phone because you want to speak with the person who is calling shows a purpose. Getting out of bed when you hear your alarm clock so that you can get dressed shows a purpose.

Despite what your purpose happens to be, it always stands its ground against a lack of purpose.

Think of the last time you walked into a room simply because you were invited by someone else. *Not a time when you were going to class to take notes, nor a time when you were attending a church service to hear the sermon being preached.* The last time you did something simply spanning from an invitation, you were where you were because someone else wanted you to be there. It was not merely because you wanted to be there. How was that different for you as opposed to being in a place where you had a purpose to be? Being somewhere or doing something without a purpose is tremendously different from when you have a purpose.

A purpose always feeds into one question: **Why?** Although *why* is only one word, it tends to boldly stand alone as a powerful question. Not only is it a powerful question by itself, but it gains even more strength when it comes together with other words. *Why am I here? Why do I want to do this? Why is this happening to me? Why is this taking place?* Questions synonymous with these often overflow our thoughts with great intensity when we are faced with troubling times. Nevertheless, one thing in life combats troubles of any size: **prayer**. Although we may overlook the importance of prayer at times in our lives, what may happen in one second of time is likely to bring forth the need for prayer.

Throughout my childhood, my mother emphasized the need for prayer. Before going to bed each night, she would take the time to kneel in prayer with me so that I would spiritually connect with God. My mother also felt the need for me to make a biblical connection with my prayers. As a result, she selected Bible scriptures for us to recite each night. She and I would speak the words of the Bible scriptures aloud with each other, followed by engaging in silent prayers of our own. This spiritual routine has had an immensely powerful impact on who I am throughout my lifetime.

Days have come about in my life when I have felt the need to kneel before the Lord and pray this simple, yet powerful prayer: *Lord, I pray that you will bless me with guidance and direction.* No matter how simple or complex your words may be, praying to God is important. Making a connection with my spirituality has served as a very positive force in my life. It has taught me the significance of many things that are especially important, yet often overlooked. Allowing the light of positive actions to shine over all situations is certainly one key lesson that I have learned. Always remember that there is a light even in the darkest situations. Instead of only looking at the flaws of a situation, look at the fine points of that same situation. Believe in your heart that the best is yet to come! "For our light and momentary troubles are achieving for us an eternal glory that far outweighs them all" (2 Corinthians 4:17 NIV).

Despite how your set of circumstances may appear, you must still see yourself in a positive light. There are times when things may appear to be too much to handle, even though you are putting your best foot forward. You may begin to feel as if you do not have what it takes to be a victor, and the thought of settling as a victim may come to mind for you. Regardless of what is happening in your life, always take the time to speak the words of Psalm 139:14 into existence about yourself: "I am fearfully and wonderfully made."

One of the best ways to build a positive light around yourself is to take the time to see your points of growth. How is the person you see in the mirror today different from the person you saw in the mirror 3 months ago? How is the voice that you express today different from the voice you expressed 3 months ago? How is the person you are today different from the person you were 3 years ago? If your answers show a better side of yourself, then you see growth within yourself already. On the other hand, if your answers show a lack of change for the better, you still have work to do. No matter how you answered these questions, rest assured that God has a purpose for you.

God made you in the manner that He made you for a purpose. He placed every point in your life where it happens to be for a purpose. The Lord has a purpose behind every set of circumstances that He places in front of you to keep a passionate fire within you. My friend, where there is no purpose, there is no passion. We must always remember this. When we face setbacks in life, it becomes quite easy to forget this.

Setbacks in life have the capability to not only make us question ourselves but to question God. *At this very moment, why am I living? What is God's purpose for having breath within my body? God, why did You even create me?* When everything is going well in our lives, we are more than likely to give positive answers to these questions. However, life's setbacks tend to steer our answers toward negative responses. Negative responses make us embrace negative choices that overshadow the greatness that lives within us.

Never let a setback cause you to make choices that will lead you to negative consequences. Declare these words to yourself: *I am who I am! Nobody will get the best of me! I will work to be the best me that God has ordained me to be!* Walking through the valley of the shadow of death may appear as a time of contradictions to your beliefs of becoming a victor, but having trust in the Lord far surpasses any contradictions that the natural eye may happen to see. Your success tomorrow begins with your trust in God today. "But without faith, it is impossible to please Him: for he that cometh to God must believe that he is, and that he is a rewarder of them that diligently seek Him" (Hebrews 11:6 KJV).

Do not let the trivial things in life control who you are. There was a day when I lost my keys at a public establishment, and I had to get a new key for nearly everything that was on my key ring. Added to this, I felt the need to have the locks at my home changed. Although this brought about unexpected financial costs, I was still able to replace what I lost. I was dealing with material items, which could be replaced. My friend, do not allow things that can be replaced to reshape who you are.

When the obstacles that we face embody large problems in our lives, it becomes a much stronger test of our faith. There are many times in life when we happen to wonder if God is truly listening to our prayers. We have periods in life when we do not receive the answers to our prayers within the timeframe that we want, and this often challenges our faith. However, the setbacks that we face do not happen without a purpose. God knows how to use your worst days to lead you toward much greater days ahead.

God's reason for allowing setbacks to take place in your life is to stimulate you out of your comfort zone. The Lord wants to spiritually provoke you beyond the status quo. Your walk through the valley provokes you to see progress. He has brought forth a thirst within you for new goals to be achieved in your life. A hunger to reach greater heights now lives within you. The setbacks you are facing today are setting you up for better places tomorrow. You cannot take steps of comfort and steps of courage at the same time. As a result, God is preparing you to courageously step beyond your challenges and reach your blessings.

Our Heavenly Father places challenges on your path for a reason. When you are confronted with a challenge, you must take a risk to move beyond the challenge. You must step out of your comfort zone to rise above your challenge. Time after time settling for the status quo is what a person feels most comfortable doing. Even so, a challenge leads to change. It does not allow you to settle for the status quo. So many people want to remain in the status quo because it is a place of comfort, and change is a part of the unknown. The unknown is a place in life that is greatly feared, even though the unknown may be the best place for us to be.

People tend to be afraid of change because of its lack of familiarity. A lack of familiarity takes away a person's comfort zone. Being in your comfort zone appears to be one of the safest places to be, but it is one of the most hindering places to be. Instead of becoming a greater version of yourself, your comfort zone holds you back from rising to greater heights. Your comfort zone is dangerous because it destroys your courage and crushes your confidence. While a challenge may seem to be something that has the power to dismantle who you are, remember that nothing has more power than God. My friend, step away from your comfort zone and follow the steps where God is leading you.

Despite what you happen to be doing in your life, there is always one thing that you need to have a purpose for before you begin to pursue it: *a goal*. Do not worry about your goal being "too much" for you to achieve, or "too much" for you to handle. Focus on *why* you are pursuing your goal. When you know your purpose for achieving your goal, it is much easier to combat challenges that come against you. By clearly knowing your purpose, you will stand strong against the struggles that come along with your goals. Let your struggles show your strength.

No goal will come without problems, but God's power combats all problems. Do not ever think that God does not have a purpose for the problems in your life. For every step that seems to move you toward success, remember that it is ordered by the Lord. For every step that seems to move you away from success, remember that it is also ordered by the Lord. The valley is a place of wilderness; it is uncharted territory. Your steps are being made in the wilderness, which is a place where we tend not to want to be. Even so, there is no need to watch your feet as you walk. God is ordering your steps. With each step you take as you walk through the valley, let these words resonate within your spirit: *The Lord is with me!* "A person's steps are directed by the LORD. How then can anyone understand their own way?" (Proverbs 20:24 NIV).

What is not understandable with our own knowledge makes sense when we allow God to direct us. There are many times in life when things would move much smoother if we would simply follow the points that God has placed for us to follow. Nevertheless, we often think we already know what is best for us, so we fight with God when it comes to where we want to be. We tend not to realize that regardless of what we *think* is best, God always *knows* what is best.

Too often in life, we are afraid of a stumble. No matter what stumbles in life may occur, we must remember to look to the Lord.

He knows what is best for every situation that we happen to face. Just because a situation is not flowing well for us today does not mean that we will not rise to greater heights tomorrow. There are times when what looks bad must happen so that what is great will happen. Times will exist when God will have us walk toward new paths in life, yet it seems as if we are still walking on the same path that we are doing our best to leave. Regardless of how it appears on the surface, always remember that God is working things out for you. Despite the oppositions that may take place in your life, rest assured that God's favor is waiting for you on His timetable.

A temporary opposition may become a long-term blessing. *No,* at one point in time, may just happen to be God's way of telling you an answer with these two words: *not now*. Let this reality resonate within your spirit. Let it echo throughout your soul. Look up to see how high you will rise, not down to see how low you may fall. Always hold strong to your faith. Never succumb to fear. Hold strong to the belief that God's greatness is surrounding you, and He is always with you. "For I am the LORD your God who takes hold of your right hand and says to you, Do not fear; I will help you" (Isaiah 41:13 NIV).

A spirit of fear makes you fall, but a spirit of faith makes you flourish. Keeping the faith that great things are ahead in your life is a constructive force, but embracing the fear of failure is a destructive force. By accepting failure in your life, then you will have failure. However, if your faith fights against failure as you trust in the Lord, then you will be blessed. With this, you will not be a failure, nor will failure linger on as a part of your life.

Think of choosing between faith and failure as signing a contract. You must look at the actual cost of a contract upon your life before you sign your name to the contract. When you see failure in your future, you are signing a contract of failure into your spirit. This will lead you down a path to follow actions that will steer you toward failure. On the other hand, when you see a future of blessings, you are signing a contract of faith into your spirit. With this, faith empowers you to trust in the Lord so that you will reach your blessings. Regardless of what your situation looks like now, spiritually sign your name to a contract of faith.

My friend, do not tear down the greatness that lives within you. With each breath that you take, build up yourself as a great creation of God. Despite the obstacles that come before you, remember that faith empowers you with the spiritual currency to confront any challenge. Nevertheless, there must be a need for you to spend that spiritual currency. In order to overcome a challenge, there must be a challenge. In order to have a testimony, there must be a test.

Faith is what you must use as the shoes that you walk in with each step you take in your walk through the valley. "Now faith is the substance of things hoped for, the evidence of things not seen" (Hebrews 11:1 KJV). When it comes to faith, there is a spiritual foundation upon which we must realize God's reasoning. One of the strongest reasons why God uses faith is to enlighten us. Our Heavenly Father makes us knowledgeable of the excellence that lives within us by prompting us to use our faith.

On the surface, a situation may seem as if it can never be accomplished. You may feel like you are walking through a dense fog that makes it more difficult to reach your destination with each passing moment. It may seem as if giving up is the best thing to do. Nevertheless, faith is a tool that makes what once appeared as if it would never be overcome to manifest into a triumphant testimony in our lives.

When we can see that by believing our current situation will become a better situation, this enlightens us when it comes to the power of faith. At the beginning of the day, it may appear as if a set of circumstances is too much to handle. With faith, the same set of circumstances may later become a testimony to the power of faith at the end of the day. By seeing this happen, we are certainly enlightened when it comes to the power of faith! We can see God's power in action through our faith, as His favor rains down upon us!

The foundation of faith is also built upon God using His power to encourage us. There are so many places on the path of life where all we want to do is hang our heads in defeat, because it appears that there is no way that we will ever conquer our challenges. In such a place, we simply want to be the victim of the situation, and we no longer want to strive toward becoming the victor. However, God brings forth points of encouragement in our lives that inspire us to continue moving forward. By doing so, He lays the foundation of faith in our lives so that we can stand strong against any challenge.

It often requires us to have life's low points for us to receive encouragement from the Lord. If everything was always good, we would not learn to appreciate the good things. We would not know the difference between a good moment and a bad one. When we can move beyond life's tough times and reach the good times, we are able to see God's power in action. Low points of life are a part of God's mixture that He uses to create the foundation upon which we stand with confidence and shine with faith.

Our Heavenly Father wants to motivate us to reach new heights instead of compromising with the current ones. God works to have us reach greater heights than we ever thought possible. My friend, no matter how big a challenge may appear, never underestimate yourself. Do not run from adversity! Conquer it!

God further molds the foundation of our faith by empowering us. The Lord gives life to courage within our souls. He shows us that there is no challenge too great for us to overcome. Despite how difficult the challenges you are facing may appear, rest assured that God will bless you to stand up again much stronger than you were before. He will allow the setbacks you are facing to make you flourish into an even stronger follower of His excellence. My friend, you must have the spiritual audacity within yourself to look your challenges straight in the eye as you hold strong to your faith!

The Lord places boldness within your spirit so that you will not face your challenges in a common, average way. You were made in a unique fashion, and God empowers you to face your challenges in a unique fashion. One of the most unique things that we come across on a consistent basis is food. Just picture how two people can cook the exact same thing, but it can taste totally different. What tends to bring forth the significant difference in taste is the seasoning given to the food. Although one cook's meal may have a sour, bland taste, the other cook's meal may have a taste that keeps you coming back for more.

Your faith is the seasoning of your situation. Faith brings forth an uncommon edge to a common set of circumstances. The faith that lives within you is a unique seasoning that you add to what is taking place in your life so that the taste of your situation shifts in your favor. One of the most common things you can do to improve the taste of a meal is to add an uncommon seasoning. The same rings true when it comes to using faith as your seasoning to bring forth greatness in your life.

Our Heavenly Father gives strength to your spirit that allows you to stand strong against your struggles and challenges. Every step toward a blessing is not a step taken with comfort. As a result, it requires courage to take a risk to reach out for your blessings. There are many times in life when we tend to feel that something is beyond our grasp. We are hesitant about taking a risk because it appears that we have too much to lose. Even so, always remember that what God has for you *is* for you. Do not fear a risk. Success starts with a risk.

My friend, the "reasoning" of the world mentally conditions you to internalize your "place," and not expand beyond the walls of limitations. It makes you feel that there is a "lane" where you must remain. However, God empowers you with faith so that you will see your success ahead. He blesses your spiritual ears to hear your upcoming excellence being shouted from the rooftops. Our Heavenly Father also imparts hope within your heart to guide you beyond your struggles.

Knowing that God will empower us with the strength that we need to be blessed shows the magnitude of His power. God is not limited to mathematical formulas, nor is He limited to scientific procedures. He spans far beyond logical reasoning, and He rises above approximated assurances. My friend, the size of the strength that God places within us provides the tenacity to rise above our challenges.

Too often when a person rises above a challenge, you will hear one word used over and over: **luck**. Nevertheless, you are not blessed merely by being "lucky." Things do not turn out in your favor by chance. God has a strategy for every step you take. He orchestrates every step you take for a reason. We do not serve a *random* God. Our

God is a *strategic* God. Every piece on the path of your life is ordained by God. It is God with you, and luck has nothing to do with the situation. Although God is with you at every moment of your life, you can certainly tell the moments when His presence is with you at an exponential power.

The blessings that come into your life have nothing to do with being "lucky." They are gifts from God. He prepares us with life experiences, then He paves the way for us to reach our opportunities. As you think about this, just remember that when God is with you, it does not matter who or what is against you. This is because God is your defender and He never has lost, nor will He ever lose. My friend, the next time you are uncertain if you will reach the opportunity that you need in your life, always keep the faith that God will bring it to pass. Faith brings opportunities in the place of oppression. Our Heavenly Father will bless your preparation to come together with the needed breaks in life that He has waiting for you.

The blessings in our lives are some of the strongest points that show us what our purpose on the path that God has us following happens to be. A blessing may be what God is using to show you how to overcome a challenge in order to expand your horizons. It may appear to be a loss on the surface, yet God is using it to move you toward greater heights in life. Circumstances in your life may look like setbacks that you will never overcome, but they may be blessings in disguise.

Regardless of how God chooses to advance us in life, He wants to see faith on our part for Him to unfold His works in our lives. Many people believe that large happenings must occur in order to overcome life's challenges. Nevertheless, God's Word shows us that this is not true. "If you have faith as small as a mustard seed, you can say to this mountain, 'Move from here to there,' and it will move. Nothing will be impossible for you" (Matthew 17:20 NIV). I cannot say enough that what appear to be small things in life make a big difference. When you know your purpose, you can take something small and make it big.

Have you ever thought about the fact that the words "problem" and "purpose" have the same number of letters? There is a reason for this, and there is a connection with it. No problem that you encounter comes into your life without a purpose. Problems in our lives often make us want to get away from them as fast as possible. As we experience problems in our lives, it seems much easier to jaywalk instead of following the right path. However, our circumstances turn out much better when we follow the right path.

The path you are following may seem long, inconvenient, frustrating, or even a combination of these emotions. Even so, always remember that despite the problems you encounter, God has a purpose for the problems. With each experience that comes forth in your life, there is a reason behind the experience. You have a reason behind each step you take on your path in life. At no point in your life will God have you move in vain. Look to the Lord for direction on your path. Travel with a purpose. Expect the best, knowing that you are the best.

There are so many days when it is difficult to hold strong to the belief that the best is yet to come in the days ahead. Some days of your life may bring forth a constant flow of tears from your eyes, because of the challenging times that are taking place. Despite this, remember that tears of today will water the faith within your spirit if your faith is merely the size of a mustard seed. Regardless of our circumstances, a key thing must live within our spirits so that we will have a connection with the power of God: *trust*.

Our trust must rest upon what the Lord will bring forth in our lives. We must declare within our spirits that because our trust is in God, greatness will manifest in our lives. No matter how pessimistic our situation may appear in the eyes of man, we must look through the eyes of faith with trust in the Lord. Never let your natural eyes overpower your spiritual eyes. Let your trust in the Lord allow your blessings to unfold. "Trust in the LORD with all thine heart; and lean not unto thine own understanding. In all thy ways acknowledge Him, He shall direct thy paths" (Proverbs 3:5-6 KJV).

I cannot encourage you enough to remember that the paths you follow in life will have highs and lows. They will have hills of hope and valleys of pain. Many people accept the belief that giving up is the only thing that can be done when a challenge comes forth. However, God did not bless you with a foundation to your faith for you not to use it at the times when you need it the most. Your spirit should never endure dark valleys without faith as your light and connection to the Lord.

To reach high points of triumph, there are low points in the valley that we must experience. The valley is not a place of comfort. It is a place where you will endure struggles that will lead you to higher ground. There are so many times when a person may see successful business owners, excellent educators, outstanding surgeons, and highly requested attorneys. Although the titles that these individuals have gained are often tremendously respected, most people do not know the struggles that these individuals have had to endure to gain these titles. Always remember that you cannot see progress if you do not rise above your struggles.

If God simply allowed you to be satisfied with the status quo, there would be no motivation within your spirit to see a change in your life. God must upset the status quo in order to bring forth a desire within you to see a change for the better. Never settle for the status quo. Do not compromise with mediocrity. Settling for mediocrity makes you accept being a mediocre person. It causes you to be less than your best. My friend, you were made by the hands of God, which should show you that you are much more than mediocre.

Walking through the valley is often a necessary point in life because it keeps us from settling for mediocrity. So many people settle in life because of the fear that where they come from will limit how high they can reach. Aiming high in life is a risk, but it is certainly a risk that I encourage others to take. My high school English teacher used to always have a quote of the week as a part of her lessons. These optimistic quotes had a beneficial effect on me during my time as her student, and they are still points of hope that positively impact me. It is amazing how we will remember quotes for years to come when they have a tremendous impression on us. Knowing this, mediocrity is certainly not something that I embrace. "Mediocrity is seen as fine only by those who are mediocre."—Anonymous

The mistakes that we make tend to steer our minds toward settling for mediocrity. Our mistakes make us want to shake hands with fear and bow down to defeat. Instead of being fearful of your mistakes, develop a positive relationship with your mistakes. Learn from them. Grow beyond them. Never forget that God has mercy upon your mistakes, so have mercy upon yourself. You are not equivalent to your mistakes. You are not equal to your worst moments. My friend, the resistance that you place against your mistakes opens doors that you never imagined you would walk through.

We have often been programmed by society to continually think about our mistakes. If you did something on your last job that caused you to be fired, what good is it doing you to think about that mistake every day? Accept it as a part of your past and grow from it. If something you did in your previous relationship caused it to end, is it benefitting you to use large segments of your time wishing it did not happen? No. Accept it as a part of your past and move beyond it.

When you spend time regretting the mistakes of your past, you waste energy that should be productively used in the present. All of this comes from the fear of how your mistakes might negatively work out in your life. My friend, fear places the belief within us that we cannot rise above mediocrity. Wondering whether we have what it takes to achieve our best often makes us want to settle for the status quo. Despite how difficult the challenges you are facing may seem, rest assured that God will bless you to stand up again much stronger than you were before.

God will turn what is a mess in your life today into a message through you tomorrow. He will transform a mistake that you made in your past into a miracle in your future. Our Heavenly Father will allow the setbacks that you are facing to make you flourish into an even stronger follower of His excellence, and a bold leader of your fellow men. "For though the righteous fall seven times, they rise again, but the wicked stumble when calamity strikes" (Proverbs 24:16 NIV).

Our Heavenly Father must provoke your comfort zone for you to have a hunger in your heart to reach goals that you once never imagined would be attained. The Lord upsets the ordinary to bring about the extraordinary. "And he shall be like a tree planted by the rivers of water, that bringeth forth his fruit in his season; his leaf also shall not wither; and whatsoever he doeth shall prosper" (Psalm 1:3 KJV). If God allowed you to always be comfortable where you are, there would be no need to walk to a better place. This is because there would not be a better place to reach. As such, there would be no valley to walk through to get to a better place.

When the thirst for reaching points of triumph exists within your spirit, you will not simply lie down to a challenge that stands between you and your goals. By looking up to the Lord, you understand that He controls days of victory and days of defeat. My friend, by looking up to God, your mindset rises higher.

Whether you have a positive mindset or a negative mindset, the way you think controls your actions. Your thoughts set the tone for your actions. With this knowledge, look to the Lord in the best of times and the worst of times so that your movement will be an advancement. "For as he thinketh in his heart, so is he" (Proverbs 23:7 KJV).

A person's mindset is controlled by one of two things: *What the person feels limited by when it comes to what he or she pursues, or the limitations that the person feels he or she has the power to overcome.* Nevertheless, *faith* is the one thing that leads a person beyond any limitation. People tend to spend so much time wondering what *cannot* be done, and too little time stepping out on faith to see what *will* be done. Wondering makes you blend in with others, but stepping out on faith makes you stand out on your own. My friend, regardless of your set of circumstances, faith is always a powerful tool to have. Faith makes a mess of impossibilities become a message of extraordinary accomplishments and testimonies when your steps are guided by the Lord. "Order my steps in thy word: and let not any iniquity have dominion over me" (Psalm 119:133 KJV).

Faith removes barriers and replaces them with bridges. When faith lives within your spirit, you know that nothing can hold you down in life. "I can do all things through Christ who strengthens me" (Philippians 4:13 NKJV). Keep in mind that faith takes you from the valley of the shadow of death and leads you to the mountaintop of triumph. Never underestimate what you can do when you have faith. Despite what is happening in your life at this very moment, always remember that God is in control. No matter where you happen to be, see the best in what you have. Embrace optimism with your expectations. Flourish in whatever the soil happens to be where our Heavenly Father has planted you.

There are times in life when we begin to believe that because we lack something now, we will always be held back from achieving our best. Do not accept this to be true. Work with what you have now to get more than what you need in the future. Where you are now does not determine who you are or what you will become. Where you stand does not determine how you stand. Where you live does not determine how you live. On the surface, it may appear that what you lack will hold you back. Turn away from this belief. Logic may keep you limited, but faith makes you limitless.

As we live our lives, we tend to come across stumbling blocks. However, a stumble is not a fall. Faith steers you back up when a stumble attempts to bring you down. When life gives you a detour, faith drives you where you need to be. Although stumbling blocks will manifest in your life, do not accept the belief that you will crash. Look to the Lord for direction, and He will guide your path.

Never forget that things move much smoother when you know where you are going. When you know that your destination is victory, your path toward victory will be much smoother. This will make your steps come from a place of victory that is led by faith. My friend, despite a stumbling block causing a twist on your path, you are still able to use your faith to steer yourself where you need to be. The valley that you are walking through is by no means a straight path, but faith ensures that you will take the steps to move beyond the valley.

From unexpected turns to congested detours, your valley is not a clear path. However, guidance from the Lord makes even the darkest points in life become clear. *Pray! Pray! Pray!* This is what I highly emphasize in the best of times and the worst of times. As you walk through the valley, you must embrace prayer as a tool that connects you to the Lord. By having a connection to the Lord, you will receive guidance along with your walk. Always remember that prayer is one of the strongest forces that gives you guidance from the Lord. Start your day in faith through prayer. End your day in faith through prayer.

Prayer is always a powerful tool that comes together with faith to overcome life's challenges. One prayer has the power to speak volumes even in the darkest hour. Never forget that prayer is not passive, but active. Applying the relationship between prayer and faith into your life makes your rough paths smooth. It turns stumbling blocks into stepping stones toward greatness. With faith, what you ask of the Lord in your challenging times will become blessings that are realized in times ahead. "Ask and it will be given to you; seek and you will find; knock and the door will be opened to you" (Matthew 7:7 NIV).

For every word that comes through us in our times of prayer, there is a reason. My friend, for every thought that produces the words of our prayers, there is a reason. God has a purpose for our need to connect with Him. Regardless of how difficult this very second in your life may appear, hold strong to the belief that God will bless you to step forward into prosperous territory. "Hear my prayer, LORD; listen to my cry for mercy. When I am in distress, I call to you, because you answer me" (Psalm 86:6-7 NIV).

Life's education is a powerful instrument, especially when it comes to being spiritually educated. Becoming educated with the Word of God steers you where you need to be and away from where you do not need to be. Being spiritually educated with the Word of God allows your steps to be taken in the right direction as you walk through the valley. By developing your spiritual education, you will become a wise follower of the Lord. As wise followers of the Lord, we obey Him and our walk through the valley is well-guided.

As prayer and spiritual education come together in our lives, we look through the eyes of faith and see the steps that our Heavenly Father is prompting us to take. With this, we must obey the steps that He instructs us to take as we walk through the valley. By following the light that God shines down upon our steps, we can see where He is guiding us. Although we go through struggles as we walk through the valley, it is a time when we see prayer empowering our connection to the Lord.

There are days when it may seem as if you are simply going through setback after setback, stumble after stumble, and challenge after challenge. Regardless of this, still remember that God has a purpose for every step that you take on your path in life. There is no predicament in which God places you without a purpose. Our Heavenly Father has reasoning behind inspiring our prayers, and faith serves as the spiritual stepping stone to bless those prayers. Your predicament may seem to be too much to bear, but never forget that a promise of victory lives within your prayers. "Devote yourselves to prayer, being watchful and thankful" (Colossians 4:2 NIV).

Keep in mind that your set of circumstances may happen to be what God is using to shed light upon one thing in your life with which you surround yourself: *people*. The people with whom we surround ourselves have a significant impact upon the challenges we overcome. Think of one person in your life with whom you are strongly connected. For the next 60 seconds, close your eyes and reflect upon this person. Now, open your eyes.

As you thought about this person, what came to mind for you? Is this someone who is supportive of you in your life's best times? Does this person also support you in your life's worst times? Is this someone who helps keep you going in the challenging times of life when all you can do is fall on your knees in prayer? Your set of circumstances may happen to be what God is using to show you that the people with whom you surround yourself are why you have or have not overcome your challenges.

My friend, one of the strongest pieces of advice that I have for you is to be careful with whom you surround yourself. Your path in life will be much smoother if you are surrounded by people who lift you up, instead of by those who tear you down. Be cautious of those who attempt to be toxic to your triumph. People who are around you have a much easier time placing their views inside of your mind, and their beliefs within your spirit. Knowing this, be careful who you allow to become close to you. Although the painful intentions of others to bring you down do not control your purpose, it is in your best interest to distance yourself from these individuals so that you will reach your destiny.

When a person encourages you, this is an empowerment to your spirit. It may seem at one point that there is no reason for you to take another step on your walk through the valley that you are enduring in life. However, being around the right people serves as a reminder that God has a purpose for the path that you are following. Surround yourself with individuals who keep optimism within your spirit. Let the people who are in your circle bring hope within your heart. Embrace others who feed a positive mindset within you. Make certain that the people around you encourage you to keep in mind that God is in control of every situation, regardless of how it may appear. Take bold steps of integrity and allow this to create generational blessings for those who follow you. Let the good things that you take in from your positive circle bless you and those after you. "The righteous *man* walks in his integrity; His children *are* blessed after him" (Proverbs 20:7 NKJV).

Always remember that our Heavenly Father's purpose has great power. Never forget that each step we take is ordered by the Lord. There are times when it seems as if no matter how much we attempt to step to the left, we are only able to step to the right. My friend, always pause and take the time to reflect upon situations like these. If you are only able to move in a different direction than the one you are attempting to follow, consider if this is God's way of showing you a better path to follow. God will provide fertile ground for you to spiritually walk on as you walk through the valley.

Changing the path that you are following is a key reason you must be careful when it comes to the people with whom you surround yourself. Some people are very encouraging when it comes to you making a change in your life. However, others happen to be quite discouraging. Always take the time to step back and spiritually examine who is in your life, why these individuals are in your life, and what these people happen to be doing for your life. Ensure that the spiritual wavelength upon which these individuals exist is beneficial to you.

Knowing that a person benefits your life is crucial when it comes to making a change in your life. A beneficial person will encourage you to listen to God when He tells you to bring about a change in your life. God's call might be for you to change your career path from a lawyer to a nurse. He might be telling you to step away from being a teacher and to become a principal. The Lord may happen to be leading you away from being a doctor and toward becoming a business owner. Our Heavenly Father may even happen to be guiding you to move to a different state to live so that you will find better prosperity.

Change is a difficult feature to accept in life. Despite God directing you toward change, negative individuals tend to spread a pessimistic view onto the new path where God is leading you when it includes change. Do not embrace the negative beliefs that others attempt to inflict upon you. Pray to the Lord for guidance when it comes to your path. Let the Lord direct you where you should be in life, not man. Allow God to lead you toward your goals. Do not just dream about accomplishing your goals. Believe you will accomplish your goals.

God will put you in a different lane in life at times, but there is always a reason behind His works. It may be your boss moving you to a different position, even though you believe that you were the best person in your former position. Nevertheless, this change may serve the purpose of God moving you to that new position to make you rise higher instead of staying at a lower place.

Our Heavenly Father has a purpose for your path, and for you being on that path. Keep in mind that God will never leave you, no matter how difficult your circumstances happen to be. Always remember that the Lord will never forsake you, despite how challenging things may appear. My friend, God spoke the very ground that we walk on into existence, so never underestimate His power to bless us to overpower our obstacles. God will turn our biggest obstacles into our best opportunities. "Be strong and courageous. Do not be afraid or terrified because of them, for the LORD your God goes with you; He will never leave you nor forsake you" (Deuteronomy 31:6 NIV).

No matter what may transpire in your life, let it resonate in your mind that God orders each step you take according to His will. There are times when we do our best to make sense of why our steps are even on the path that we are following. Even so, it may not make any sense to us, whatsoever. Despite this, instead of attempting to bring forth logical reasoning to God's plan, simply put your trust in God's plan. Keep in mind that our Heavenly Father applies excellence to your journey in life, no matter how it may seem on the surface.

Analyzing one step on your path in life with natural logic may make it appear as if failure is the only result that will come to you. On the other hand, trust in the Lord illustrates that the one step you do not understand may be what God is using to make you soar into greatness. Imagine for a moment that one step on your path in life happens to be walking out of a hospital after learning that you have a disease. During that time in the hospital, picture yourself having become knowledgeable of your blood type. Now, envision that you have become a testimony of God's greatness by winning your battle with your disease. Take it a step further by visualizing that a close friend needs a blood transfusion after a car accident, or this friend will die within a matter of hours.

Visualize yourself hurriedly taking steps into the hospital where your friend happens to be. Picture yourself being able to quickly donate blood on your friend's behalf. As a result, you will save your friend's life all because you became knowledgeable of your blood type during a time when you had a health scare. The step that was a part of your walk through the valley in your life that brought forth learning about your blood type made no sense by itself. However, it made perfect sense when paired with being able to donate blood to a dying friend. A situation like this reflects God supplying needs in your life for a test that revealed a disease within you to become a testimony in your life. Also, it shows God supplying you with knowledge that provided your friend with a need. "But my God shall supply all your needs according to his riches in glory by Christ Jesus" (Philippians 4:19 KJV).

There are times in life when we forget that the blood of Jesus covers us in all our circumstances. *When problems come about in your life, have you tried Jesus as your spiritual solution? In the good times of life, have you tried Jesus? In the bad times of life, have you tried Jesus? My friend, in all times of your life, you must try Jesus!* With Jesus as your guide, you have the power to surpass any obstacle and move beyond any challenge that comes about in your life. With Jesus as your Lord and Savior, you gain the much-needed direction that we all need in life. Regardless of your situation, Jesus has the power to bless you to overcome any adversity.

When you look to the Lord for direction, you will find your purpose on the path that you are following in life. Establishing a connection with Him makes you gravitate toward greatness, and it sets the tone for triumph in your life. My friend, fuel your faith by studying the Word of God. Strengthen your faith by praising God. Reach out to the Lord with praise.

Pray to the Lord with a mindset of progression toward your blessings. As you enhance your connection to God, a spirit of expectation will begin to live inside of you. With this, you will boldly believe that God is in control of all situations. When you know that God is in control, you will wait for your blessings with a spirit of expectation, not doubt or uncertainty. "I waited patiently *and* expectantly for the LORD; and He inclined to me and heard my cry" (Psalm 40:1 AMP).

God tests your faith during the times when you are waiting to receive your blessings. By holding strong to your faith, you will embrace a spirit of expectation. No matter how badly a situation may appear to the natural eye, faith brings progress to what appears to be an unbeatable situation. When it is the right time for you to receive your blessings, they will come to you. Regardless of how difficult your circumstances may appear, praise the Lord for your expected blessings. Let your faith stir up expectation within your spirit so that it will keep motivation within you. "In the morning, LORD, you hear my voice; in the morning I lay my requests before you and wait expectantly" (Psalm 5:3 NIV).

Reflection is one of the most powerful, thought-provoking exercises that will strengthen your faith and empower your spirit as you wait for your blessings to materialize. My friend, try an exercise of reflection with me. Write down what is bothering you at this very moment. Next, write down the blessings that you want to come to pass in your life soon.

My Reflections:

____

____

____

____

Following this, close your eyes for the next sixty seconds and reflect upon what you have written. Let your mind think deeply and carefully about what you have written. Now, pray over what you have written. *How do you feel now? Do you sense a difference within yourself? What was it like being able to put what has been on your mind in writing, and then placing power over it through a time of reflection?*

Placing mental power over your obstacles is one of the most effective things that you can do. This allows your mind and spirit to come together on your side. When obstacles enter your life, stand up to your obstacles. Announce to your obstacles: *You will not get the best of me!* Declare to your challenges: *You will not get the best of me!* Believe in your heart: *No problem will ever get the best of me!* By embracing strength within your spirit, you will empower your spirit.

Praise our Heavenly Father in advance for the greatness that will come to pass in your life. Keep in mind that praise is what you give God in the best of times and in the worst of times. Never let the obstacles in your life stop you from praising God. No matter how things may appear on the surface, always know that your praise to the Lord is your weapon against all obstacles. Let your praise to the Lord combine with your spiritual exercise of reflection. Enable prayer to be a regular activity in your life, while you let your faith stand its ground over the obstacles that you may encounter.

My friend, I want you to create a practice for overcoming your problems for the next 7 days. As you did in the earlier exercise, set aside a time for reflection and prayer. Take the time daily to write down the problems that are present in your life. After this, write down the blessings that you want to receive from our Heavenly Father. Close your eyes for sixty seconds. Envision yourself moving beyond the problems that you have written and receiving the blessings that you have also written. Speak to God through prayer in connection with what you have written. Finish by opening your eyes and thinking about how you feel after your time of reflection and prayer.

Regardless of what problem may present itself in your life, take it in stride knowing that God is in control. You are alive because God is in control. You still have a chance because God is in control. You can be a better *you* because God is in control. Let your eyes of faith rest upon any point of trouble in your life so that it will become a triumph! Step out on faith, knowing that nothing is impossible when God leads you.

It is so easy to step aside from your challenges because of the past. What we did not accomplish yesterday is a strong factor as to why we hesitate today, or why we will not even make the effort tomorrow. Doubt leads you to entertain the idea of failure. Do not let doubt pollute the possibilities that you have in life. Do not allow doubt to supersede the greatness that lives inside of you. Smell success when you wake up in the morning. See a victor when you look in the mirror. No matter what has taken place in your life, always remember that each day is a new day. Never let a bad experience define who you are.

God reigns over your problems and your blessings. He reigns over the best of times and the worst of times. Just as your accomplishments are ordained by God to take place, the problems in your life are also ordained by God to take place. You would not have a valley to walk through if the valley had not been approved by God to be in your life. Accepting this reality was a point in my life when my faith began to flourish. I was able to see that faith brings progress to what appears to be an unbeatable situation.

Regardless of what happens in our lives, we must remember that every point of life comes with God's approval. Nothing that happens in life takes place without God allowing it to occur. Although excellence and blessings are ordained by God, also know that obstacles and challenges are ordained by God. He allows each thing in our lives to take place at every second in time where He places them for a reason. As you keep in mind that God controls all points of our lives, let this encourage you to pray with expectancy. Let your heart beat with encouragement, not discouragement. Let the seed of faith take root in your spirit. Keep a smile on your face even on the days when it seems like you will never win the race that you are running.

Life shows us the reality that we will all have a valley to walk through. The valley brings forth a humble spirit, as it takes away a spirit of pride. In some of the worst times of my life, instead of holding my head down in defeat, I strengthened my connection with God. I kneeled before Him in prayer. I sang songs of praise, and I did everything I could to connect with Him. Hold your head high as you endure days of excellence, as well as when you endure days of sorrow. Let your vision be guided by faith. The eyes of faith are a formidable opponent for failure.

Failure often has a good friend: *your fellow man.* This is why spiritual caution is necessary. My friend, making your issues known to man is not a requirement of your faith. Simply fall on your knees and go to the Lord in secret prayer when you do not see a proper spiritual friend. Leave every burden that you have before our Heavenly Father with the faithful confidence that He will work things out in your favor. At the same time, if you do find someone who you see as a spiritual partner, take the time to spiritually connect with this person. During your time together, draw this person closer to God, and come closer to our Heavenly Father yourself.

As you walk through the valley of the shadow of death, hold strong to the belief that you are walking through low points to reach higher ground. This tends to be difficult to believe when things appear to be taking a long time to happen in your favor. Times in our lives will come about when our Heavenly Father allows the same thing to take place repeatedly so that we will learn new lessons from the same message. When God shows you something a second time, He is showing you something that you did not see the first time. It is like reading the same sentence repeatedly until you come across one word that changes the entire meaning of what you have read. Looking at that one word may be something that speaks volumes. Without that one word in the sentence, the entire meaning of the rest of the sentence would change. Sometimes it takes a lack of words to make us understand what is being said in the entire sentence. The same rings true in our life experiences.

With each moment of understanding, as we walk through the valley, time begins to paint itself as a particularly important factor in our lives. Time is not something that God has placed in our lives as an enemy, yet this is often hard to remember. Giving up may often seem like the best thing to do when your point of success appears as if it is taking too long. You may wake up thinking: *This is taking too long!* You may go throughout the day thinking: *This is taking too long!* You may go to bed thinking: *This is taking too long!* Nevertheless, remember that God's time is always the right time. There are times in life when God will take you on the longer route the first time around so that you will appreciate the shorter route the second time around.

Our lives may even have points when God will have us take two steps back so that we will take five steps forward. You may not have a job after countless interviews, because God is telling you that you should be your own boss, not someone else's employee. Perhaps job after job will not work out because you are not meant to be an employee. Your lack of employment at one point in life may be God's way of making it known that you should take a skill that you have and turn it into a successful business of your own. What appears to be a shadow over your life is not always a dark spot. The way something appears at first glance is not always how it will be. My friend, God's calling on your life may not be what you initially thought it would be. That is why you should always take the time to step back and spiritually evaluate what is taking place in your life.

Life is often seen as a puzzle. Although one piece may fit perfectly in one spot, it may not fit at all in another spot. While you may try repeatedly to have one piece of your life's puzzle fit in a particular place, your efforts may not produce the results that you want to see. You must remember that God is who organizes the puzzle of our lives. Despite how things may appear to fall apart at one point in life, rest assured that God is effortlessly placing them together at another point. God has a time for our blessings. My friend, never forget that even the darkest night has a new day. Keep in mind that a season of struggle tends to lead to a season of success. "There is a time for everything, and a season for every activity under the heavens" (Ecclesiastes 3:1 NIV).

Imagine going to work and putting forth your best effort each day you are on the job. Nevertheless, you are soon informed that you have been fired. To clear your mind, you happen to stop at a popular coffee shop on the way home. While inside, you decide to take a leap of faith. In doing so, you set the stage to take the knowledge and skills that you gained from your previous job and open your own small business. Within a matter of months, you turn your small business into a multimillion-dollar corporation. This happens because of your networking abilities coming together with your knowledge and skills gained from your previous position.

In a situation like this, keeping in mind that you went from an everyday employee to a millionaire because of a risk you took after being fired would speak greatness over the power of faith. Situations like these show us that when one point of life appears to be breaking down, it may be building up. It often takes God breaking something down that we are content to settle with so that we will build up to greater heights. Too often we want to settle for less than the greatness that exists within us because we are afraid of something in life that could be our best friend: *opportunity*.

Never be afraid to answer the door when opportunity knocks. Always be ready. Do not let fear overpower you. Do not allow fear to paralyze the steps you take on your path in life. Fear is the bold enemy of faith. For you to let faith overpower fear, faith must live at the center of who you are. The next time an obstacle presents itself before you, ask yourself this question: *Is faith a random footstool in my life, or is it the foundation of my character?*

For you to stand strong in the valley, you must be able to stand strong during your life's worst times. Instead of bowing down to a challenge, stand with confidence in the face of the challenge. Never let an obstacle cause you to let go of what you know you can accomplish. "The ultimate measure of a man is not where he stands in moments of convenience and comfort, but where he stands at times of challenge and controversy."—Dr. Martin Luther King, Jr.

Pause with me for a moment. Picture yourself walking through a park while surrounded by countless gigantic trees. *How are trees that are several feet tall able to surround patrons in a park for numerous decades? What brings about their large size? How are the trees able to reach such excessive heights?* It all comes down to one thing: *a seed.* Although a seed is very small, it can produce magnificent results. Knowing this, what must be done on your part for you to see magnificent results enter your life? My friend, you must sow a seed.

While it only takes faith the size of a mustard seed to bring greatness into your life, that seed must be sown to see it blossom. If you simply held a seed in your hand, you would never see it flourish into a tree. Without planting the seed into the soil, how could it flourish? The power of what happens when you sow a seed speaks volumes. My friend, it requires action on your part to see greatness in action. If you only think about the greatness that lives within you, your greatness will remain a thought and nothing more. Put works with your faith so that you will see blessings manifest in your life. "For as the body without the spirit is dead, so faith without works is dead also" (James 2:26 KJV).

The inspiration that we need to bring forth action and fuel our faith will come forth when we least expect it. There have been days in my life when I still held onto a small amount of faith, despite just wanting to give up. Although I only had a small amount of faith existing within my spirit, bursts of encouragement came forth in my life. From unexpected phone calls to in-person meetings, I was blessed to have individuals come into my life who helped me reach my goals. I have repeatedly had blessings rain down upon me, even when only a small amount of faith lived within me. With that small amount of faith, I was able to take actions that led me to my blessings.

No matter how complicated your set of circumstances may appear, it only takes a small amount of faith to overcome the obstacles you are facing. My friend, the Word of God declares that you only need faith the size of a mustard seed. God brings great things forth, even though they begin with small things. Your high place on a mountaintop of victory begins with faith that only requires being the size of a mustard seed.

Why does God only want to see you with a small amount of faith, yet He will take this and allow you to grow exponentially? Our Heavenly Father wants us to see that great things will come into our lives, despite us only putting forth the small requirements that He asks of us. When we sow the small seeds that God wants to see us spread so that we will receive our blessings, God will exponentially bless us with more than we could ever imagine. Keep in mind that small things become great things when faith lives within your spirit. Experience is a big factor in life that shows this to us.

Experience is a part of life that teaches us more about blessings than we often realize. Our life experiences are a powerful tool that God uses to grant us spiritual maturity. Even one life experience has the capacity to sow seeds of greatness that will excessively affect our lives. My friend, one experience in your life may cause you to take a step toward reaching a goal, and it has the power to bring forth faith within your spirit to believe that it will happen. Although you may have thought about pursuing a goal that has been on your mind for many years, all it takes is one life experience to push you in the direction needed to reach it.

Life experiences serve as strong lessons that God uses to teach us why we are taking the steps that we take. God shows us our purpose on the path that He has us following so that our steps will be ordered according to His Word. When you embrace God as the leader of your path, you are no longer doubtful of your purpose of living. He makes us aware of why we are on one path in life instead of another. After you can answer ***why*** you are on your path, another critical question must then be answered: ***How should I follow my path?***

Chapter Two

THE POWER OF DIRECTION

How? This is a very strong word that can boldly stand alone as a question. It can stand by itself, yet it stands with great power. Nevertheless, it gains even more power when it is placed with other words. *How should I follow my path? How will I get there? How did this happen? How will it take place?* These are the types of questions that come about with the word **how** for the purpose of steering your spirit toward the Lord. When you are with the Lord, you are led by the Lord. With the Lord surrounding you, it does not matter where the steps you take happen to be. He will guide your steps.

When you feel full, go to the Lord. When you feel empty, go to the Lord. Always go to the Lord. Too many times in life we want to make it appear as if we are waiting on an answer from God, but our ears are already plugged with our own answer. The problem in a situation like this is that we are hindering ourselves from hearing God's answer. My friend, you cannot let what God has to say to you fall on deaf ears when He speaks to you. Take the time to be reflective. Open yourself up to the Lord. Connect with the Lord so that your spirit will gain direction. Allow questions to come to your spirit so that God can answer them for you during your time of self-reflection.

Who am I? Where am I? Where am I going? How will I get there? Why am I going there? Self-reflective questions such as these often emerge within us as we take the time to define who we are. The answers that come to these questions have a defining nature that gives power to the direction that we follow in life. On the surface, these may appear to be simple questions to answer. However, we must realize that our answers carry a large amount of weight when it comes to defining who we are. With this in mind, we must be very careful when answering such self-defining questions. Knowing this, we must look to the Lord to grant us answers to the questions that come to us during our time of reflection.

My friend, I want you to take the time to give substance to the foundation of how you define yourself personally. For the next sixty seconds, close your eyes and reflect upon each of the previously presented questions: *Who am I? Where am I? Where am I going? How will I get there? Why am I going there?* Now, open your eyes. Was it difficult for you to answer these questions? Which question was the easiest to answer? Which question was the most difficult to answer? Why is that?

There are so many things that you can often define in the blink of an eye. However, there tends to be one thing in life that is the most challenging for you to define: *you*. When a person asks who you are, what is the first thing that comes to mind as your answer? Do you believe your answer truly defines who you are? Do you illustrate yourself in the minds of others with this response? Does this response sincerely encompass what you are, or does it establish limitations upon you? When *I AM* starts a sentence in your mind, you are painting the picture of who you are to yourself. By speaking a sentence with *I AM* to others, you speak what you believe you are into existence.

Speaking to God and learning His Word serves to answer an important question for you: *Who am I?* I cannot say enough how much we often think we have our answer to this question ready and waiting to give. Even so, this tends to be one of the hardest questions to answer when we take the time to answer it. Knowing this, we must be very careful when answering such a self-defining question. Taking the time to shape who you are is one of the most productive things that you can do with your time because it ensures that you know yourself.

At points in life when we know what something is, we also know what it is not. The same rings true with you. My friend, when you know who you are, you also know who you are not. When you know who you are, you know what you will do. At the same time, when you know who you are, you also know what you will not do.

Never try to be anyone else. Be who God created you to be: ***you***! When you know who you are, you will follow a clearer path toward where you are going. When you know that you are blessed, your path toward your blessings becomes clearer. When you know that you are more than a conqueror, you will conquer your challenges. By embracing a blessed definition of yourself and a positive view of who you are, a concrete spirit of certainty will come to life within you. Taking hold of the positive definition of who you are makes you rise above limitations that attempt to hold you down.

What makes many individuals choose to drive on a road that has been in existence for many years as opposed to another road that has recently been finished? Certainty is often the main reason for this. When someone drives on a road where many others have already driven, the person has certainty about the starting and stopping points that are there. On the other hand, when someone drives on a newly constructed road, a lower level of certainty tends to exist.

For an individual to gain a higher level of certainty when it comes to a new road, it requires the person to become familiar with the road. The person must get on the road and drive on that road to make this happen. However, the fear of driving in unfamiliar territory is something that restrains many people to one area, as opposed to venturing out into new areas. What is often overlooked is that it takes someone rising above fear to have new areas to even be built, let alone for individuals to even have the choice to be there.

When you gain confidence in who you are, fear is not an impeding factor in your life. Fear of the unknown should not be something that stops you from venturing out into unfamiliar places. When you put your trust in our Heavenly Father, you can see that He has the best path already mapped out for you to follow. What the Lord has prepared for your prosperity will become a blessing for you, regardless of where it may be. "For I know the plans I have for you," declares the LORD, "plans to prosper you and not to harm you, plans to give you hope and a future" (Jeremiah 29:11 NIV).

Do not run from a path because of the pain that comes along with it. Make plans to walk in accordance with the path that God has set for you to follow. Always remember that God will bless your times of sorrow to become times of success. Dark skies of sorrow will be overridden by the sun of hope that awaits us in our days ahead. My friend, when faith lives within you, the sun will rise in your life and bring light over dark times.

Too often we become consumed with worrying about how what is happening today will become better tomorrow. Our Heavenly Father has already drawn the coordinate plane of our lives down to each dot that makes up every line. Instead of lacking the confidence to spread your wings, embrace the certainty that our Heavenly Father will bless you no matter where you happen to be.

Picture this with me for a moment. It is your first time driving on a newly constructed road. You were familiar with another road, but you decided to take a different route. However, the turn where you need to exit is closed. How could this be? What are you going to do? In your mind, you are now thinking, "I knew I should have just stuck with the road I already knew. This is too much for me!"

My friend, just because one exit on a new road where you are traveling is closed does not mean you will not reach where you are meant to be. Perhaps one exit on your road of travel is closed because God wants you to take another exit so that you will reach a better destination. While we may have one route of travel in mind, God may have a different route in His plan for us. "For my thoughts are not your thoughts, neither are your ways my ways," declares the LORD. "As the heavens are higher than the earth, so are my ways higher than your ways and my thoughts than your thoughts" (Isaiah 55:8-9 NIV).

The direction that we are traveling in has tremendous power over our lives. When we travel in the direction that our Heavenly Father has prepared for us, we are able to surpass low expectations and rise to high expectations. Spiritual direction from the Lord pushes deterrence aside, and it keeps you on the proper path that He has set for you. As we use faith as an inspirational tool, we embrace God as the light that guides our lives. By following the Lord, we are empowered with proper direction, and we avoid misdirection. What is seen as a detour in our eyes may happen to be a normal spot of travel on the path where God has placed us. Although a place on your path may appear to be a detour, it may be leading you to your true destination.

Just as *direction* in life is powerful, *misdirection* is also powerful. Imagine you are driving on a road headed east, yet you are supposed to be headed west. At the very moment when you see a "Do Not Enter" sign, you suddenly crash into another driver. All of this would be the product of you driving in the wrong direction. When misdirection exists in life, it is because we lack guidance. When we have guidance, we have direction. Knowing this, we should continually look to God for guidance.

One of the most powerful links for us to receive guidance from God is to gain an understanding of His Word. With knowledge of the Word of God, we can better understand our Heavenly Father and His works. When we understand the Word of God, we have knowledge. When we have knowledge, we have direction. When we have direction, we have power.

Our spiritual power is a needed tool in our lives that ensures that we will not enter doors that Satan attempts to open with his temptation. My friend, the Word of God is the ultimate weapon against Satan. No matter what tricks Satan may try to use to steer us in the wrong direction, our knowledge of the Word of God will keep us going in the right direction. As we learn the Word of God, we put strength behind our own words as we speak to God in prayer. By having a spiritual connection to God, we know who we are, and we know where we are going.

By lacking an understanding of the Word of God, we lack a connection to God. Without a connection to God, we are misled in many areas of life. A lack of understanding of the Word of God is a strong factor leading to misdirection in life. With misdirection, it may seem as if the more you move toward achieving a goal, the further you move away from accomplishing it. If you are on a path of misdirection, this is a very deterring element when it comes to defining who you are. To help keep yourself on the proper path in life, pray these simple words to God: *Lord, bless me with direction.*

There are times in life when instead of studying the Word of God to gain understanding, we study the words of others. With the Word of God, we have certainty. Nevertheless, with the words of others, we have opinions. The words of others tend to have a negative influence upon who we are when we give them power. My friend, when you allow the words of others to gain an influence upon your life, you give them the spiritual pen to write the definition of who you are. As this happens, you give control of your thoughts to others.

By allowing others to control your thoughts, you easily give them power over you. Just focusing upon another person's views of who you are for a matter of seconds gives them control over your mind, even if it is only for that matter of seconds. Do not do this. God made you in His image. You should be concerned with how He sees you, not how others see you.

Time and time again we focus on how others see us. *What if he thinks I am weak? What if he does not like the way I am handling this? How will she feel if I try this? How will she feel if I do not try this?* Instead of overwhelming yourself with questions of how others view you, positively define who you are and boldly accept this definition within your spirit. Knowing this, there is one person I want you to place more focus upon in the future: *you*.

Let your focus rest upon yourself, not proving yourself to others. There will be others who recognize the excellence within you. However, because of their jealousy of you, they will hope that your excellence is not something that you will also recognize. It is one thing to give constructive criticism, but it is entirely different to only give criticism. When the vocabulary of others tends to mainly center around words like *no, not, will not*, and *never,* you need to reconsider if these are people who you really need to be around. Some people want to be successful themselves in the same areas as you. Even so, they feel that there is not enough room at the top for success. With this, they may do their best to lower your self-esteem, and only get you to see the negative aspects of a situation and of yourself.

It is easy to find someone who can tell you why they think something will not happen for you. On the other hand, it is much harder to find someone who can tell you why they think something will happen for you. Although it is often much harder to find optimistic people, do your best to bring optimistic people into your circle. Do not surround yourself with people who are doubtful of who or what you will become. Surround yourself with people who are confident of who and what you will become. Surround yourself with people who will tell you why and how something positive will happen. When you are around others, concern yourself with ways you can help each other, not simply how you see each other.

My friend, always remember that you are groomed with God's grace. Do not lessen yourself based on your situation or the opinions of others. For you to move beyond the valley, you cannot focus on what others think of you while you are in the valley. Never see mediocrity when you look at yourself. When you look in the mirror, do not hang your head in self-pity and say, "I am stressed." Look in the mirror and confidently declare, "I am blessed!"

Many people often comment that I smile for no reason. What they do not realize is that on some of the days when I have smiled the most, I have endured the most pain. Despite that, I let my positive attitude rise above negative happenings. I take the gifts and talents that God has given me, and I allow myself to expand to greater heights with them, no matter how things appear around me. As I embrace optimism within my spirit, I can positively define who I am.

You must be able to define who you are so that others will *not* define who you are. My friend, when a positive spiritual definition stands next to your name, you can flourish in the best of times and the worst of times. You may be thinking to yourself, "If this process is so easy, then why is it so hard for me?" Although you have the formula for how to solve the problem, it is still up to you to use the formula to solve the problem.

Solving a spiritual problem often parallels solving a math problem, yet faith plays a pivotal part when solving spiritual problems. While some problems may seem easy to solve, others often come with much more difficulty. There tend to be days in life when our circumstances introduce us to things that far surpass who we originally believed we were or what we originally believed we could do. Everything may appear to be against you at times, but these are things that have the power to bring out the strongest side of you.

When your set of circumstances appears to be against you, step back and take the time to spiritually analyze what is taking place. Too often when a situation appears to be against us on the surface, it is because we are not looking at what God is showing us. It may seem like you have remained at a closed door for a prolonged period of time, and nothing has happened in your favor. Even so, one closed door may be what God is using to direct you toward another door that He has opened in your favor.

Imagine for a moment that it has been your dream for many years to become a nurse. Despite this, you are now receiving rejection letter after rejection letter from every nursing school where you have applied. How could this be? You have poured your heart and soul into your dream. Why is God rejecting your passion for nursing?

At times when it appears that nothing is greeting your dream but closed doors, step back from the situation to see what is taking place. Is God moving your dream aside so that He can show you a better path, or is He testing how much you want to live out your dream? Meditate upon what is taking place. Speak to God. Study His Word. Our Heavenly Father may happen to be showing you that nursing is not the best path for you to follow. He may be using your setbacks in one area as a setup for higher achievements in another area. In a case like this one, God may want you to select another path in the medical field other than nursing. While you may want to be a nurse, it may be in God's plan for you to be a pharmacist.

My friend, do not simply see a closed door in one area as the end of your path. A roadblock between you and the place where you currently think is best for you may be what God is using to steer you toward a place of greater heights than you imagined. Not every step that you will take on your path in life will be smooth. There may be times when you will want to hang your head in shame and give up when it comes to what you are doing. You may even ask yourself: *Is my walk through the valley in vain?*

Instead of looking down in shame, look up with confidence. Let the power of faith reside within you. Allow this to encourage you to see that better days are awaiting you, and these days of your life will overpower the challenging times you are currently going through. Hard times tend to bring out our anger on the inside. Do not give life to anger. Give life to hope. Inhale faith and exhale fear. Let faith come into you, and let fear go out of you. When you have faith, your worries will decrease, and your confidence will increase. Faith will fuel motivation within your spirit. Have faith in the fire of your spirit!

Let your motivation give life to positive expectations. Envision greatness for yourself and you will believe it before you see it. Knowing this, you *will* believe it *when* you see it. No matter what obstacles you may face, always know that there is a blessing ahead of you. Despite how things may seem, remain confident.

There have been times in my life when I have seen God bring about pauses to show me something that I needed to see before being blessed. I remember a day when I was walking toward my car to drive to a scheduled meeting. Barely any sign of rain existed, but it began to rain. To ensure my safety, I came back inside and turned on the television. After doing so, I found breaking news interrupting regularly scheduled programming. The breaking news significantly caught my attention due to what was happening. Shortly after this, I glanced outside, and I saw that the rain had stopped. I could see God's power in action drawing me back inside before going to the meeting. What I saw on television provided me with information to alter my decision, which was significantly helpful for me. This allowed me to be blessed before I even realized it.

As you walk through the valley, remind yourself that God has blessed you before, so He will surely bless you again. Walk with a confident spiritual posture with the steps that you take. Hold strong to the joy that you have on the inside. Just as Jesus gives you joy within your spirit, remember that He also gives you blessings. No matter how worrisome your present times may seem, always keep in mind that our Master has wonderful times ahead!

There are many times in life when we may meet obstacles that do their best to tear us down. Even so, we must allow our faith to give us the strength to rise above any obstacles that we may face. My friend, faith turns obstacles into opportunities. When faith is alive within your spirit, you will trust our Heavenly Father to direct your steps. Always remember that when you trust in the Lord, He will allow your life to flourish with blessings. Despite how your circumstances may seem, trusting God prompts triumph over pain. Embrace trust in the Lord when you speak to the Lord. Your mouth will speak with words of confidence when you trust God. Your heart will meditate with confidence when you trust God.

Let a blessed assurance be the foundation of your prayers. Pray with confidence. Embrace boldness within your spirit. Let your spiritual audacity flow through you as you ask God to enlarge your territory. People get excited about the Super Bowl so often. NFL athletes on team after team want to be players on the team that wins the Super Bowl. Nevertheless, do you think the same NFL athletes who win the Super Bowl are the same individuals who do not believe they are good enough to even be professional athletes in the NFL? *No.* To achieve an accomplishment such as winning the Super Bowl, many beliefs must stand behind that accomplishment.

Before being an NFL athlete who can set one foot on the field where the Super Bowl will be played, you must first believe that you will stand out to college scouts as a high school athlete. This belief must be enhanced by having the certainty that you will have the skills to stand out enough to play in a vast number of your college games. On top of this, you must have confidence that you will be drafted by a team in the NFL. Assurance must then exist within you to the extent that you believe you can win normal games as a professional athlete in the NFL, in addition to the necessary games that will lead you to the Super Bowl. Finally, you must believe that your team will win the Super Bowl.

Walking off the field as a winner of the Super Bowl seems to be too big of a dream for some, but nothing is too big for God. Remember that God placed the idea of even having the first Super Bowl into someone's mind before it even existed. Knowing this, He can bless you to win whatever it is in your life that you need to win! Whenever something seems to be too big of a blessing for you to have, keep in mind that God had the power to bring the universe into existence. In this regard, He has the power to do anything!

What is the "Super Bowl" in your life? Achieving it may appear to be too much of an accomplishment, but always remember that nothing is too much for God! No dream is too big for God to bless you to have! No goal is too far out of your reach. No belief is too big for God to make a reality! "But let him ask in faith, with no doubting, for he who doubts is like a wave of the sea driven and tossed by the wind" (James 1:6 NKJV).

Points in life tend to exist when we feel like it is safer to limit the goals that we pursue because of the challenges that we are likely to face. A challenge can be a very intimidating point along the path toward reaching a goal. Confronting a challenge is a risk that many people do not want to take. Standing up to a challenge takes stirring up courage within your soul, which is a challenge within itself. Regardless of what your challenge happens to be, never bow down to it. Put forth your best effort to conquer it.

Pause with me for a moment. Think of the last time that you pursued a goal. What challenges presented themselves to you? Did you confront those challenges, or did you bow down to them? What was the outcome of the situation? Are you pleased with the outcome? If you had the chance to confront those challenges again, would you take it? Why or why not?

My friend, never view a challenge as something brought forth simply to stop your progression in life. Do not merely view a challenge as a wall placed to stop you. View your challenges as tools that God uses to bless you to rise above the status quo. The challenges you face are God's way of allowing you to flourish, not fail. To fret is to have fear of failure, but to have faith is to have assurance that the Lord will bless you.

Facing a challenge will bring out fear within us if our trust does not reside in the Lord. Fear is a factor in life that tends to make us settle for less than what we are capable of becoming or capable of having. When we give life to fear, we give power to failure. Do not let this happen to you. Instead of settling for the status quo, take the risks needed to reach your blessings. Do not live stagnant. Let your trust in God make you take the risks to rise above your comfort zone.

It is easy to imagine reaching our triumphs, yet it is much more difficult to pursue them. Although a triumph is something that is easy to envision, it is often challenging to achieve. All types of problems stand between what we dream will happen and what happens. My friend, you cannot hide from the problems that come forth in your life. A problem does not become a triumph when you hide it in the shadows. Just because something is hidden in dark places does not mean that it does not exist. You must gain the courage to face your problems head-on in order to overcome them.

Times in life may exist when a person can turn a problem into a point of prosperity, but the person does not. The mere *possibility* of something not working out in life may make a very capable person give up. Do not let this be you. Just because one way does not work does not mean that no way will work. You can take a different path as long as you know where you are going.

It may seem as if the clouds in your life are hanging so low that you cannot even see the steps you are taking as you walk through the valley. Never let this cause you to give up. Remember that God will turn the darkness of the midnight hour into the brightness of high noon when your trust resides in Him. Your good days in life will always speak louder than your bad days. "Every valley shall be raised up, every mountain and hill made low; the rough ground shall become level, the rugged places a plain. And the glory of the LORD will be revealed, and all people will see it together. For the mouth of the LORD has spoken" (Isaiah 40:4-5 NIV).

Despite how difficult a situation may seem, never forget that God is still on the throne. He reigns over every problem and every blessing. The Lord wants you to take steps that are driven by faith. The actions that you take should reflect your belief that God will work things out in your favor. If there is no action on your part, there will be no attraction between you and your blessings. If you want triumph to be a point in your future, plant the seed of faith, and open your heart to receive victory. Look beyond your obstacles and look at your challenges through the eyes of faith. View the trials that you are facing as what you know will become testimonies.

Treat your obstacles as learning opportunities. View the obstacles that cross your path as a way for you to improve yourself for the days ahead of you. In life, we have opportunities to learn repeatedly. There is never a point when a person knows everything that there is to know. Only God knows everything. Whether good or bad, always remember that God blesses us with experiences in life to expand our knowledge.

I cannot say enough how many times I have seen individuals who want the storms of life to pass as quickly as possible. There is nothing that they want to learn from their experiences, nor do they have a desire to ever have such experiences again. If a person knows that tomorrow morning is likely when their current problems will end, then the person tends to rush time to pass as quickly as possible. Whenever the problem is likely to end, the person wants time to quickly pass to that point. However, despite how much a person may want a life experience to pass as quickly as possible, there is one thing in life that you cannot get back: *time.*

Time is a valuable gift that we are only given once. There is not one second that we will be able to live again once it has passed. My friend, always remember that you only have one life to live, regardless of how your days may appear. Despite only having one life to live, once is more than enough if you do it right.

Pause with me for a moment to spell *time*. T-I-M-E. Despite *time* being a word that only has 4 letters, it speaks of an infinite number of happenings. Knowing this, do not let your current set of circumstances deter you from better happenings in the future. Never let yourself be stretched too thin by your set of circumstances. Take the time to spiritually connect with our Heavenly Father to see all the greatness that He has in store for you.

Enjoy what is happening in each moment of your life. Let today and every day be a day that you appreciate. Let this second of the day be a moment of the day that you appreciate. Treat the present like a present. If you spend time worrying about what has already passed, you will not be able to enjoy what is happening now. For every second that you spend worrying about what may or may not happen as a result of your past, you will lose one second of what is already happening. Embrace the present. Love your life. Live your life. Your past is a period of your life that has already passed. Realize that your past is gone. Leave yesterday where it is…in the past.

Today is **today**, so concentrate on **today**. Love today for it being today, no other day. Your success today will not come from focusing on yesterday or concentrating on tomorrow. To be blessed today, you must focus on today. Today's blessings will come today, no other day. When you allow your mind to focus on today, this will lead you to a better tomorrow.

Do not use unnecessary energy thinking about what did not work out in your past. Focus upon what is happening now, so that you will move toward new heights in your future. Be at peace with your past. By doing this, you will embrace the present and prepare for the future. Do not accept the belief that God's best works for you happened yesterday. Embrace the belief that He is preparing a path for you today, and He has excellence awaiting you in your days to come.

When the sun rises on a new day, do not ruin it by allowing it to be overshadowed by yesterday. Release yourself from the baggage of the past. Let it go. Look forward, not backward. Move forward each day with faith and expectancy in your steps. If something did not happen yesterday, it was not meant to happen yesterday. On the other hand, if something did happen yesterday, it was meant to happen yesterday. Never forget that God is the author of our lives. When He writes the pages of our lives, He often turns some of our worst stumbles into our best steps.

Times will exist when you will stumble to a lower point from where you are so that you will rise to a higher point from where you were. Days will come about when you must have minus two at a particular point, so that you will have plus eight at another point. Although stumbles in life will take place, faith ensures that we will stand tall against them. No matter what stumbles occur in your life, trust God as the author of your life. Points of life may come about that make you want to embrace doubt. Instead of doing this, let faith do its work in your life. Faith delivers you from the incarceration of your insecurities because it makes you trust God as the author and finisher of every page of your life. With the great power that God has to make page after page come together to comprise the chapters of your life, rest assured that He has every page under control down to each letter.

My friend, when God includes something in a chapter of our lives, it was meant to be included in that chapter. When He leaves something out of a chapter of our lives, it was meant to be left out of that chapter. The Lord wants us to learn from yesterday, prepare for tomorrow, but live for today. When each new day comes, rise and shine with hope in your heart, strength in your spirit, and peace within your mind. By doing this, you will properly embrace the days of your life.

What makes you fall on your knees in prayer instead of holding your head down with the shame of failure? How are you able to keep going when it seems like everything is telling you to stop? My friend, do not give yourself a tough time because of your shortcomings. Know that you are a work in progress, not a finished product. Do not see yourself as pitiful. Embrace yourself as a prayerful work of God's power and know that your prayers will take you to great places. Look ahead knowing that a positive outcome has already been determined for you. Stand strong with joy in your heart today, regardless of the challenges you are facing.

Something that people tend to have a problem with is wanting to say that they believe one thing, but having doubt dictates their mindset so that they believe the exact opposite. You cannot be a believer and a doubter at the same time. Think of it this way. I cannot believe that my car is going to turn left and right at the same time. By having belief in what you know God will bless you to have, you allow hope to overpower your doubts. Do not cry in hopeless wonder. Smile with immeasurable faith. When you believe, you embrace peace. When you embrace peace, you embrace power.

There are times in life that exist when it seems as if the more you pray to God, the more you hear silence from our Heavenly Father. It seems like you are praying, but nothing is happening. It is as if you are only expressing voiceless words that God does not hear. Nevertheless, always remember that faith gives a voice to the voiceless. Faith is a strong force in life that speaks every language. Take the time to stop and listen to what God is allowing you to hear from Him. What may appear to you as silence from God may essentially be His way of leading you to a blessing that is much better than the blessing that you expected. My friend, see the silence of God as the Holy Hush that He is using to bless you in a way that you initially would not have considered if things had gone one way instead of the other.

If you are standing in one place where you hear nothing, take the time to step away and move to another place. If you move to another place where you receive direction and guidance from the Lord, you will see that what you thought was where you should be was not the place for you. Points in life when it seems as if God only replies to us with silence allow for a strengthened connection with Him. When you are a follower of our Heavenly Father, the faith within your spirit serves as a driving force behind your prayers to Him. The voice that speaks within you, and through you makes it known that God is at work behind the scenes on your behalf.

Do not just hear God. Listen to God. His silence is often used to prepare you to listen. The experiences that God places before us serve as some of the most powerful forces that inspire us to listen to Him. Our Heavenly Father does not need our help. We need His help. God does not have a question mark for Himself along with the collective words that make up why you are walking through the valley. Our Heavenly Father is not inquisitive regarding His own actions. He knows why you are where you are, what is happening while you are there, how long you will be there, and what the outcome will be.

Never forget that there is a purpose behind why you are where you are. Even when you pray over and over to God to move you to another place, yet you remain stalled at one place, God has placed you at your point for a reason. Despite it feeling as if you are in a place where you disagree with being, it is the best place for you to be when God wants you to be there. No matter how difficult your place in the valley may seem, it is only temporary. You will not dwell there permanently. You will walk *through* the valley. The Lord is paving the way for you to walk through a clearer path so your spirit will reach a better place. Knowing this, get out of your own way and follow God's way.

No matter how smoothly things may turn out for us after being stalled at a certain point, a stalled point tends to be a very uncomfortable situation from which to move forward. Finding your place in an uncomfortable situation is one of the most difficult things to do. Even so, stalled places are on the map of the valley through which we must walk. Regardless of how difficult a stalled point on your path appears to be, remember that no point exists without God's approval. Places of this nature are present so that God will enrich the power within your spirit.

Be at peace with God's purpose. Let the knowledge that you are God's child spiritually echo within you, and keep in mind that God wants the best for His children. Do not let your purpose differ from God's purpose for you. When you are in one accord with God, you open yourself to receive the blessings He has for you. A spirit of fear is not what God has given you. Power is what the Lord stirs up within your spirit, so that your faith will supersede worries that do their best to hold you down. Although you will walk through the valley of the shadow of death, you will walk with spiritual peace when you are guided by the faith that God places within you.

Having faith does not mean you will not face troubles in your life. When you have faith, this means you will have the needed tools to overcome the troubles that you encounter. Hard times do not define you unless you give them the power to define you. Even when you are the underdog, never settle for accepting the idea that you will lose your battles. Trust that God will use your situation to make you become the best of the best. My friend, you are more than a conqueror! "For our light and momentary troubles are achieving for us an eternal glory that far outweighs them all" (2 Corinthians 4:17 NIV).

God puts hope in the hearts of His followers. Where the word "hopeless" stands, God removes the suffix "less" from its root "hope," so that "hope" is what stands strong. Despite your set of circumstances, remain hopeful for better times to come. Let hope within your spirit overpower doubt within your mind. Hope feeds the hunger for belief. When you believe you can do something, you open the door for it to happen. My friend, when you believe you are a victor, you pave the way for your steps into victory.

As you walk through your valley, listen to the sounds of your footsteps. Listen to what God is saying to you with each step you take. Not only this, take the time to understand why God makes you take each step you take as you walk through your valley. Ask yourself: *What is the story behind my walk? What is the purpose of my walk? How does one step of my walk influence another? Why do I continue to walk through the valley even on days when it seems that my steps are getting me nowhere?* My friend, when you can answer these questions, you will be able to clearly take the steps you need to take so that you will walk beyond the valley and stand tall at the mountaintop of triumph. Build a connection with God for your answers. Study the Word of God for your answers. Keep the faith that God will provide you with your answers.

Be careful not only how you walk, but also who walks with you. Many people are so eager to stand beside you after you have taken your place at the mountaintop of victory. However, these same people very often lack the desire to walk beside you as you take steps on your walk through the valley. A person who we believe is helping us may very well be holding us back. These individuals may make you embrace the view that you do not have what it takes to achieve something in life. This is why I strongly encourage you to be very careful when it comes to the individuals who you allow into your life. One word is a key aspect of life that people who will hold you down will bring into your life: *fear*.

When you wake up in the morning, do you accept yourself living in a place of faith or fear? As you walk through the day, do you accept yourself as living in a place of faith or fear? When you lie down at night, do you accept yourself living in a place of faith or fear? Many people live in fear because of projecting the negative things that may happen in place of the positive things that may happen. Do not let an incarnation of fear dictate your thoughts or control your mind. While fear makes the winds of a storm even more powerful, faith brings peace of mind in place of chaos. My friend, what is in you is either standing in the way of what is in front of you or opening the door for what is ahead of you. It is up to you to decide which will live within you…faith or fear.

Fear has held so many talented people back from using their talents. Instead of avoiding taking a shot in life because of the fear that you may miss it, take the shot with the faith that you will make it. Look at your situation through the eyes of faith, not from a point of pessimism. Do not go through life thinking about bad news that may come. Despite the bad news that may exist, good news still exists in your life. Regardless of how things may appear, just speak these words: *It is well!*

Always be careful about who is around you. The people around you may be key points of encouragement in life-and-death situations. I once had the privilege of meeting a woman with quite the story to tell about standing up to fear, and showing how important others are when it comes to helping you do this. Her doctor informed her that she had a serious health problem, and it was very unlikely that she would live beyond the upcoming months. Nevertheless, when man says something will not happen, faith speaks the power of God into action for it to happen.

Although she could have listened to her negative health report and given up, she did not allow this to be the outcome of her life. This woman walked beyond her health problems into a place of inspiration that motivated her to become a nurse. During her battle with her health issues, day after day she saw nurses provide such great care for her to the extent that she wanted to become a nurse. The nurses not only provided great care for her but also encouraging words daily.

Within months, her doctor began to see dramatic changes in her health. Soon after, he was shocked to see that a complete turnaround for her health had taken place. When she was informed that she no longer had the health problem with which she was previously diagnosed, tears of joy began to roll down her eyes. This was a woman who heard in the previous months that she likely would not live beyond the months ahead, yet God said otherwise. Overcoming the results of the test that the doctor previously reported to her became a testimony of the power of God in her life.

Once she was able to return to her normal life, she thought of the nurses who provided her with such outstanding health care and powerful words of encouragement. Resulting from this, she knew that she wanted to be an individual who would provide others with such awesome care and inspiration. This fed into her passion to become a nurse. She talks constantly about what a pleasure it is for her to get up and go to work each day to help her patients. This woman sees her career as a blessing to her patients and herself.

Moving beyond health problems may be the valley through which God has placed you to walk. Whether it is a small health issue that has entered your life or a large problem with your health that you must overcome, your valley may be an issue of health through which God has placed you to walk. When I think of a health issue that affected an exponential number of people, the coronavirus comes to mind. The entrance of this pandemic into the lives of millions of individuals throughout the world served as a time in history when God stepped in so that we would honor and understand a very important scripture: "Be still, and know that I am God; I will be exalted among the nations, I will be exalted in the earth" (Psalm 46:10 NIV).

From financially prosperous countries to those with economic deficit, it was as if data resulting from the coronavirus was reflecting a pandemic that could not be controlled. Looking from a natural standpoint, it seemed as if the best thing to do would simply be to give up if you had even the slightest thought that you contracted the coronavirus. Businesses that were financially flourishing prior to this pandemic began to shut their doors in massive numbers due to financial shortfalls. Schools were forced to bring a halt to in-person education as a result of the problematic effects of the pandemic.

It appeared that the coronavirus was a global problem that could not be overcome. This natural pandemic exerted its power with great force. Nevertheless, we serve a *supernatural* God. We must remember that the coronavirus could not have come about without the approval of God. Knowing this, I held strong to a significant Bible scripture when I would see news reports surrounding the coronavirus: "No weapon formed against you shall prosper" (Isaiah 54:17 NKJV).

Whether it is a global pandemic or a minor problem to overcome, hold strong to the belief that God will not allow anything to prosper against you. My friend, no matter what is happening in your life, keep the faith within your spirit until the last second of the battle that God is in control and on your side. Let the Lord order your steps as you walk through the valley, no matter how challenging things appear to be.

A situation does not defeat you. Your response to the situation is what has the power to defeat you. If you could simply wait until you saw what you wanted to happen in your life, there would be no need for faith. Think of it like watching a game. Games in various sports often make millions of dollars and have millions of fans watching the games. Fans tend to watch the games in person and on television with the desire to see what the outcome will be. Although one team may be the winner "on paper" and the other team may be the "underdog," fans will still put their full focus into the game.

As you watch a game, you are often on the edge of your seat waiting to see what will happen. It may appear as if one team will beat the other team hands-down, but you keep the faith that the team you want to win will win. Now, imagine that you are playing in the game. Picture it as if the game is coming down to the last second and your score is about to win or lose the game. Why don't you simply give up? Isn't it all too much? *No.* You do not give up. You give it your all. Why? It is because of one word: ***faith***.

My friend, no matter what the situation that you are in happens to be, do not let doubt take over your mind or depression take over your spirit. When you allow doubt and depression to define who you are, you allow worry to lead each step that you take. Worrying is simply an action that wastes time, and it holds you back from achieving your best. In order to move forward in life, God must lead your steps. He allows hope to be your shoes. You must hope for better times ahead, not allow worry to gain a place in your mind. God does not worry. He puts His will into action. Instead of worrying, rest assured that God will put His will into action in your favor. There must be unity between you and God for you to see His works in action. Open yourself to His guidance, and trust in His will.

The steps that you take will not always move down a smooth, straight path. By spiritually embracing the hand of God, you can see His power in action. When you follow God, He will make crooked places straight, even when your steps become harder for you to take. Our Heavenly Father may have to take you out of your normal element to bring your greatness into action. The reality that your steps appear harder to take may be because God is shifting how you are walking. Your steps may seem to be hard to take as you walk because God may be changing the path that you are following. "I will go before thee, and make the crooked places straight: I will break in pieces the gates of brass, and cut in sunder the bars of iron" (Isaiah 45:2 KJV).

As you walk through the valley in your life, look up to the Lord with optimism, not down with defeat. Regardless of what your valley happens to be, keep the faith. Always know that faith brings healing to you, no matter how difficult your hardships happen to be. Stand in agreement with God. Know that He has the power to heal you even when man says no healing is possible. My friend, troubles are temporary, but God is legendary. His power is permanent. Despite how your situation may appear at this very second, hold strong to the belief that God will work it out in your favor.

Times in life may seem so tempting to look back at what has placed you where you are, instead of focusing on where you are.

When your focus rests upon the here and now, you can flourish where you are. Not only that, when you flourish where you are, greater things begin to blossom in your future. What is happening in your situation does not mean that you are buried below more than you can handle. It means that you have been planted in a place where you will bloom. Think of it this way. Let us say a nail just got in your tire, and now you are on the side of the road with a flat tire. Does it benefit you more to think about how the nail got in the tire, or does it benefit you more to think about changing the tire? If your focus is on changing the tire, you are preparing yourself for advancements ahead of you. However, if your focus rests on how the nail got in your tire, you are keeping yourself at a standstill. My friend, what is in front of you far outweighs what is behind you.

Optimism and pessimism do not co-exist. You cannot be optimistic that something will happen and be pessimistic about it at the same time. Faith cannot drive your spirit along with fear, doubt, and worry. Have faith at this very second, not doubt. Keep faith in your life. Not a few minutes from now, not tomorrow, not a few days from now, but right now. When faith lives within you in the present, it is much easier for it to remain within you in the times ahead. With each day we live, we tend to want things to take place just the way we want them to be. However, this often is not the case. Walking through the valley is certainly not something we want to do, and our steps through it do not always go the way we want them to go.

Despite this, the way out of the valley is through the valley. To get through the valley, we must have faith.

There have been times in my life when I have felt like everything was going against me. It felt like the more I stepped one way, the more I was pushed the other way. I would wish that certain points in my life would rewind, fast-forward, pause, or stop to help me so that I could take better steps. Even so, I soon learned that despite how the steps that I was taking appeared at first, every step I was taking was being taken for a reason. Life has no rewind, fast-forward, pause, or stop buttons. What God means to happen will happen. What He does not mean to happen will not happen. What He means to allow you to revisit will come again for you to revisit if that is His will. Pay attention to the spiritual narrative being written in your life by God with each step you take as you walk through the valley so that God's guidance will be much easier to grasp. As you walk through your valley, declare that your steps will not be made in vain.

We are often closest to reaching our blessings when we endure the most challenges. Others may look at your situation and have nothing but negative things to say about it. They may not understand how you could possibly have faith that God will work things out for you when an overflow of negativity appears to display itself in your life. Your faith may be a misunderstanding to others, but an understanding to you. With faith, your set of circumstances at this very second may sincerely turn your situation around and push you into a triumphant blessing that others never would have expected you to have. "But without faith it is impossible to please him: for he that cometh to God must believe that he is, and that he is a rewarder of them that diligently seek him" (Hebrews 11:6 KJV).

Faith is a powerful tool that steers us in the direction where God leads us. You may wake up tomorrow morning only to learn that you have been passed over for a promotion at your current place of employment. *What would you do?* That would certainly serve as a situation of being able to see the glass either half full or half empty. The same amount of water is in the glass, but the way you view the water is what matters. Always keep in mind that the way you view a situation is what steers you toward what will happen next.

With faith, you do your best to refill the glass of your life. Without faith, you pour out what is left in the glass of your life. As an optimistic person, you are steered toward actions that will make the glass of your life overflow. Nevertheless, as a pessimistic person, you are steered toward actions that will make the glass of your life become empty. My friend, having not received a promotion that you deserve could steer you to use the gifts and talents that you have to open a business of your own and become a wealthy business owner. Imagine that being the case, and one day a person comes into your office at the business that you started after being passed over for a promotion at your previous place of employment. The person may ask what inspired you to open such a successful business. One word would be on the tip of your tongue: *faith*.

There are so many people I know who are successful businesspeople who felt the need to refill their glass of life after God steered their direction through faith. A woman once told me that she was sure she would advance at a company where she previously worked due to so much time and effort that she put into her job. She would arrive early, give it her all during business hours, and stay for long periods after she was off the clock. However, on the day when the owner announced the person who would gain the promotion at the company where this woman worked, she was stunned. The employee who gained the promotion turned out to be a man who had only been with the company for a few months, and who also had much less experience than she did.

After leaving the meeting, she took the time to reflect upon what happened. Her knowledge and experience were being taken for granted, not to mention she was being financially compensated at a much lower rate than her coworkers. With this, she made up her mind that night to quit her job and become her own boss. Having only been in existence for a small number of months, her business began to profit hundreds of thousands of dollars. At the same time, her previous employer was able to see that he made a very bad decision by not promoting her. Without her working for the company, it soon began to endure a significant financial loss.

To stop his company from continuing to have such a loss, her previous employer contacted her attempting to bring her back to the company. Added to this, he proposed that he would provide her with the promotion that she previously wanted. Nevertheless, she turned his offer down. To this very day, her business still sees great financial prosperity. It is now worth more than the company where she previously worked. None of this would have ever been possible if she was not overlooked when it came to the promotion she wanted. When she stepped out on faith to become her own boss, the promotion at her former place of employment became a mere afterthought. "Take delight in the LORD, and He will give you the desires of your heart" (Psalm 37:4 NIV).

As shocking as it may seem, a situation in which a person's gifts and talents are overlooked at a place of employment tends to be the motivating factor that the individual needs to move toward a blessing. Along with this, faith is what prompts the person to step out toward that blessing. There are many people throughout history who would never have become great businesspeople if things had gone the way they wanted them to go on the job. So many people who financially struggled at their previous places of employment are now able to help others with their financial needs. My friend, although you may suffer during your walk through the valley, keep the faith that you will reign as you stand on the mountaintop! "For the LORD thy God blesseth thee, as He promised thee: and thou shalt lend unto many nations, but thou shalt not borrow; and thou shalt reign over many nations, but they shall not reign over thee" (Deuteronomy 15:6 KJV).

Direction in life is one of the best things that we can have. How can you walk somewhere when darkness is all around you? It is because a light still shines through you from your faith, and this allows you to know where you are going. You can walk in darkness when you know where you are going, but not when you do not know where you are going. How do you know where you are going? You must have guidance. Look to the Lord for guidance. Our Heavenly Father gives us guidance in life, no matter how our situations may appear. He uses our faith to shine a light on the path for us to follow. The Lord directs us in the best of times and the worst of times. My friend, despite how your circumstances may appear, keep the faith.

Picture yourself in a dark room in your place of living. Why can you still move from one place to another with confidence even though you cannot brightly see the room? It is because you have direction. Although you do not physically see what is where at the time, you can see it in your mind. Always pray to God for direction and look to Him to gain direction.

One of the most powerful ways that we can gain direction in life is by showing thankfulness to the Lord before He even gives it. Do not be ungrateful to Him for what you do not have. Be thankful to Him for what you do have. When you learn to appreciate what you have, God will bless you with even more. This is because you will appreciate your blessings, instead of taking them for granted.

My friend, another thing is a key part of gaining direction in life: *belief*. It is one thing to believe when things are going your way. However, it is entirely different to believe when you are going through difficult times that make your blessings look as if they are a million miles away. In the best of times and the worst of times, what you believe sways your direction. It is not where you come from that matters in life. It is what you make of it. Keep believing!

Although you cannot physically see the outcome of your situation now, if you know where you are going, you will get there when you have faith in the Lord and the belief that He will take you there. Think of getting in your car to drive to a restaurant where you want to purchase a meal. Do you just get in your car and begin driving? Of course not. You have a plan for where you will go, and you have a strategy for how you will get there. When the sky is as clear as daylight, you have a plan to reach your destination. When the sky is dark at nighttime, you still have a plan to reach your destination. When rain pours down during a storm, you still have a plan to reach your destination. Some of the most difficult days of our lives are times when God shows us the power of a plan. It is especially useful to have a plan when times get hard. On a rainy day, it is empowering to already know where you are going.

Your dream becomes your plan, and your plan becomes your pursuit. Regardless of how things look, let your belief stay alive! You were built to break the mold. You were built to defy the odds. For that to happen, you must believe that it will happen. "Commit your way to the LORD; trust in Him and He will do this" (Psalm 37:5 NIV).

You cannot expect to be blessed throughout the day when you lose faith in the morning. Business may be slow but remember that God did not simply put the idea for your business in your mind for it to merely become a failure without a fight. A bad health report may have been recently delivered to you but remember there is no illness that God cannot heal. Whatever the valley that you are walking through happens to be, never underestimate God's power to bring you through it. Believe in the power of our Heavenly Father. As you walk through the valley, boldly declare these words: *My miracle is coming!*

I cannot say enough that if everything always worked in your favor from a direct standpoint, there would be no need to have hope in your heart. If every step you took in life was a step that you could clearly see was on the path where you wanted it to be, there would be no need for you to believe that greater times are ahead of you. Your walk through the valley is not simply leading you away from times of chaos in your life, but also toward times of greatness ahead of you. The steps you are taking today as you walk through the valley are testing your faith. Nevertheless, your test today will be your testimony tomorrow.

One of the strongest ways that a person can express a testimony is to speak it into existence before it even happens. Express aloud what you believe. By speaking aloud what you believe, you spiritually legitimize your beliefs. Speak your blessings aloud so that you will listen to them and internalize them within yourself. Speak life into your blessings.

Although blessings become closer to us when we speak them aloud, fears are often spoken aloud more than blessings. Fears are one of the most active things that a person speaks. Even so, you cannot speak of your faith and fear at the same time. The two cannot hold power in your life together. Remember that faith is the foundation of your testimonies because it leads you to your testimonies. Let the words that you speak coincide with faith, not fear.

Before you let even one word come out of your mouth, keep in mind that you are allowing what you are saying to have influence over your life. *Is there something that you should be careful about verbalizing? Are you communicating something aloud that you should not? Do you need to come to the Lord in prayer about something that you are thinking, instead of giving it life through words that you are speaking to others?* Reflect upon questions such as these the next time you wonder if you should speak something aloud. My friend, let the words you speak allow faith to flow through you, not fear to overpower your mind. "Even a fool who keeps silent is considered wise; when he closes his lips, he is deemed intelligent" (Proverbs 17:28 ESV).

You cannot speak about how much faith you have that God will work things out in your favor, and at the same time speak about how much fear you have that the situation will not work out for you. Do not speak your words with a spirit of fear. Speak your words with a spirit of faith. The best way to gain peace of mind is by making what you fear become irrelevant. When you verbalize your fears, you speak defeat into existence. Let faith overpower fear in your life. When you think about financial issues, combat these thoughts with the basis of Deuteronomy 15:6 by speaking these words aloud: *I will lend and not borrow.* When you think about health issues, combat these thoughts by speaking aloud the words, "I shall not die, but live, and declare the works of the LORD" (Psalm 118:17 KJV).

My friend, I want you to take part in a regular spiritual habit. Close your eyes and search your heart for the blessing that you desire. Speak the blessing aloud. Claim your blessing with your beliefs and have faith that this blessing will become *your* blessing. Speak aloud daily that this blessing will be *your* blessing. Let the words of your mouth connect with the desires of your heart. When you speak, a voice of victory should echo through you. Victory cannot have a voice when it does not live within your spirit. Look to the Lord with the belief that the possible will overpower the impossible. Always remember that Jesus proclaimed that even though things may be impossible with man, all things are possible with God.

Speak positive things into existence about yourself by saying them aloud from the first-person point of view. Do not speak aloud from the third-person point of view with words such as, "You are successful." Declare affirmations from the first-person point of view with words such as, "I am successful." Wake up in the morning, look in the mirror, and let yourself know that the world needs you. Speak these words into existence: "I am here for a reason! God has blessed me with breath in my body for a purpose! I am not worthless! I am worth it! This is a day I am living because God is doing something with me!" My friend, do this to change your state of mind for the better so that you will empower your spirit, enhance your beliefs, and strengthen your faith.

With faith, the impossible becomes the possible. The possible then becomes reality. There have been times when I have spoken to others who have told me that they felt the need to just quit when it came to their goals in life. Do not allow such a mentality to overtake you. If great things were not still ahead of you, breath would not still be in your body. Instead of looking back, look forward. Instead of looking down, look up. Instead of being quiet about what God has done for you, praise Him for what He has done for you. When things seem to be too much for you to handle, just speak these words to yourself: *I WILL DO IT!* My friend, no matter what *it* happens to be, spiritually declare that you *WILL* do it. Believe in your heart that you *WILL* do it. Hold strong to the hope that you *WILL* do it.

By replacing the words *never* and *can* with the word *WILL* in your vocabulary, changing your mentality is one of the most powerful things that will happen. Your life situations tend to be the easiest things that naturally place the vocabulary of who you are within your mind, but you must make sure that those words positively coincide with your spirit. You may have had what appears to be one of the worst days you have experienced recently. Even so, finding an outlet to positively express yourself is something I highly encourage you to do to overcome this. Writing is a way that God has blessed me to positively express myself, as well as a way for me to touch the lives of others. I do not merely write for the masses. I write for someone who will pick up this book, read the words on the pages, and be inspired.

Always know that God steers your direction with His power. Look to the Lord for direction. If God meant for you to be doing anything else at this very moment, that is what you would be doing. My friend, you are reading the words on this very page of this book for a reason. You are reading this book in the location where you are reading it for a reason. God would not have even placed the idea in your mind for you to open this book if He did not have a purpose for you to do it. No matter what is happening in your life right now, never forget that God's power is guiding your direction.

Chapter Three

BLOSSOMING WITH BLESSINGS

hallenging. Restless. Aggravating. Words like these often burst into our thoughts when we face setbacks in life. Today it may seem like there is nothing more in the place where you have been planted but problems. You may feel as if you have done everything in your power to triumph over your troubles, but there is nothing left to do but give up. Nevertheless, God's power is much greater than our power. There is no challenge that you cannot overcome when you put your trust in God. Instead of falling in frustration, look up to the Lord with motivation. The soil where you have been planted may seem like it has nothing in it but problems, but it is still a place where you will prosper when you trust in God. Regardless of where you are planted, you will prosper there when you trust in our Heavenly Father.

Times exist in life when it appears that only darkness fills the sky. You may feel that despite closing your eyes to darkness at one point, you still open your eyes to darkness at another point. When darkness seems to be what clouds your spirit, step back and look at what God is showing you. Perhaps He is using what is taking place in your life as an experience to humble your spirit, instead of allowing you to overflow with pride. Perchance your situation is one that the Lord is using to show you the strength that lives within you, which you were previously not aware existed.

Although the sun sets to end one day, it also rises to begin a new day. When a new day comes, new opportunities come. With new opportunities come new methods to move beyond obstacles. We must always remember that no obstacle will defeat us when our faith rests in the power of the Lord. By opening your eyes to a new day, God is showing you that great things are ahead in your life. Let optimism rest within your spirit, despite how things may appear to the natural eye.

Approach your challenges with a proactive mindset. Think to yourself: *My challenge is already conquered!* Believe in your heart: *I have already won!* Declare to yourself: *There is no challenge too big for me!* Let the words of Romans 8:37 ring out within you: "Yet in all these things we are more than conquerors through Him who loved us." Proclaim it! Own it! Believe it! My friend, the hunger for victory must live strongly within you. Although you will be confronted with challenges in life, the fire of relentlessness must burn through you.

The best way to truly believe that you are more than a conqueror is to have faith live within your spirit, regardless of the circumstances. With faith as the foundation of your spirit, you embrace the belief that God brings advice to the anxious and counsel to the confused. Faith silences the anxiety within your spirit when you are faced with challenges. When faith lives within you, it empowers you to take a bold stand in the face of adversity. On the other hand, when fear lives within you, it holds you back through the limits of doubt. My friend, what lives within you is what is expressed through you. Let faith live within you so that you will put on the full armor of God and stand your ground against any challenge that may come before you. "Therefore, put on the full armor of God, so that when the day of evil comes, you may be able to stand your ground, and after you have done everything, to stand" (Ephesians 6:13 NIV).

One thing in life brings about a true test of who you are: *time*. I cannot express enough how much time is something in life that illustrates for you a portrait of the *true* you. We often do not realize that a delay in our time happens to be the *right* time in God's time. One important thing about time is that what we can handle now may happen to be what we were not able to handle in the past. Additionally, what we want to happen now may be something that we are not able to handle yet, which may be why God is delaying the receipt of our blessings.

When it comes to your walk through the valley that you endure, time is often the tool that God uses to strengthen you. Things that appear to be difficult and challenging today may be simple and easy in the days to come due to what has happened with the passage of time. Something may exist in your life at this very moment that seems to be too much to bear. However, God is having a season of your life serve as a time when you walk through the valley to show you that nothing is impossible to overcome with Him as your leader. As you walk through the valley, God is preparing you to prosper, not wither. No obstacle comes before you without our Heavenly Father providing you with preparation for it. Keep in mind that God did not call you to walk through the valley without equipping you to walk through it.

God's plans do not always match our plans, nor does His time always match our time. Even so, God's works always have greatness behind them. Although the Lord brings forth hard times for us to endure at certain points in life, He uses His force to make us rise to greater heights. Our Heavenly Father uses the difficult times in our lives to show us that we are more than conquerors. When we see that we can conquer challenges today, we will remember that we are able to conquer challenges tomorrow. My friend, let the good things that God guides you to do today empower you to gain a harvest of greatness in the days to come. "Let us not become weary in doing good, for at the proper time we will reap a harvest if we do not give up" (Galatians 6:9 NIV).

God not only chooses the valley where you walk, but He also chooses the soil on which you walk. The soil on which you walk may make it seem like you will never walk out of your valley. However, the soil where God places your spiritual feet to take the steps you take in your valley shapes who you are. God is selective of the soil on which He places your feet. With each second that passes, God has you where you are for a reason. Our Heavenly Father wants you to be in a place where you will flourish.

In my personal walk through my own valley, my spiritual feet were so heavy that I could barely put one foot in front of the other. The soil on which I walked seemed to be too much. It felt like I was in quicksand. Despite what was happening, I kept walking. I made up in my mind to continue my journey so that I would know what the end would be. The faith within me made me realize that God's works were working through me. No matter what was taking place around me, I held strong to the belief that God had better days coming forth for me to see blossoming.

My friend, you are a seed of God's works. Just as rain falls upon a seed for it to blossom, it must also fall upon you so that you will blossom. God has you in the right soil with the right amount of rain falling upon you at the right time so that you will see your blessings when you blossom. Although the rain that falls upon you in the valley may appear to be too much to bear, always remember that you will tremendously blossom at the end of your present circumstance. "You gave abundant showers, O God; you refreshed your weary inheritance" (Psalm 68:9 NIV).

Although we tend to love our lives when the sun shines, the sun will not shine every day in our lives. If every single day of our lives was only filled with sunshine, it would dry us out. It would reduce what we have to offer. We would have no appreciation for sunshine because we would have too much of it. There must be rainfall for blossoming to occur. When you blossom, God makes it clear that you are His blessing in action. As a blessing from God, you go from being a small seed in the soil to a massively tall tree.

Never merely view where God has placed you from a negative standpoint. Although you may be going through hard times, keep the faith inside you that you will rise in the end. Do not view a downfall as an insult, but an inspiration. With faith, what appears to make you fall will make you spring high. Faith will lead you to the highest mountaintop, with great lessons learned after you walk through the lowest valley.

God allows the happenings in our lives to come about so that we will rise far beyond our expectations. Never succumb to the belief that a goal is too big for you to accomplish. Do not hang your head in defeat when things appear not to be going well. My friend, so much *can* happen in a mere second. With this in mind, we must hold strong to what *will* happen when we have faith. When faith resides within your spirit, mountains are moved.

You may be financially struggling and unemployed when driving into the parking lot of a bank with the intention of passionately appealing to the manager to extend the date of your car payment. Those around you may have taken out small loan after small loan to help you, but your financial needs are just not being met. Within seconds of pulling into the parking lot, you could receive a phone call informing you that you have been selected to fill the position for which you interviewed yesterday. Also, the bank manager may give you the needed car payment extension. Weeks later as an employed individual, you could go from having been someone who previously needed financial assistance to being someone who gives financial assistance to those in need.

Times exist when we want to understand every twist and turn that comes about in our lives. When this does not happen, worry tends to make its way into our minds. Instead of being at peace with what is taking place in our lives, we become overwhelmed with the uncertainty that exists from the standpoint of the natural eye. However, if we could simply see and understand everything taking place in our lives, there would be no need to have confidence in the power of God. If we understood every point of every day, there would be no need to trust in God. My friend, do not focus your energy toward understanding all the days of your life. Let your energy rest upon your trust in God.

The challenges we face may appear in the eyes of man as bad things, but God tends to use them as setups for great things ahead of us in our lives. Remember that when we follow God, He always takes us to great places. As we follow God, He creates a trail for us to follow with each step we take. Do not try to understand your steps from the standpoint of our Heavenly Father. Trust God to be God. Trust God to direct your steps. When your trust resides in Him, He will give you direction and show you your purpose. "The steps of a good man are ordered by the LORD: and he delighteth in his way" (Psalm 37:23 KJV).

Every step that you take as you walk through the valley has a purpose behind it. My friend, you must look at what God is showing you during your walk. Although He is using certain points to clearly illustrate things to you as you walk, others are not seen quite as clearly. As you walk through the valley, be sure to check your blind spot. There may be something God is showing you that is not directly in front of you. One of the main things that your blind spot may show you is the significance of timing. Something may be *for* you, but it may not be for you at a *specific* time.

Having you walk through the valley may be God's way of having you check your blind spot before making a significant turn in life. Checking your blind spot when driving is often overlooked as a small act. However, this seemingly small act *avoids* millions of accidents in everyday life, but it *leads* to millions of other accidents when it does not take place. As you check your blind spot, you will see things that God is showing you that otherwise would never have stood out to you. With this, you will trust God to lead you through the valley instead of trying to follow broken paths of your own.

During a time of spiritual reflection, a verse from Psalm 23 empowers me when it comes to my walk through the valley. "He maketh me to lie down in green pastures: he leadeth me beside the still waters" (Psalm 23:2 KJV). When times become rough for you, keep in mind that even though you are walking through a valley, God still has a place of calmness in your life. He has a place of calmness within your spirit even during the difficulties that you are enduring.

Being led beside still waters brings balance into your life, regardless of what is happening. Despite the many ways you could be walking as you walk through the valley, pay attention to the reality that God is guiding your steps beside still waters. It may appear to the natural eye that what you are going through is too much to bear, and no step that you take will allow you to progress. However, looking at your situation through the eyes of faith allows you to see balance with how God is ordering your steps.

Having your steps led by God makes you resist the distractions of man. Many people may not understand how you can walk through a valley in your life, and still walk with the divine favor of God guiding your steps at the same time. No matter how tumultuous the valley in your life happens to be, still waters are there to keep balance present for you. My friend, you may not understand why you are walking through the valley where God has placed you, but keep in mind that God will allow an explanation to pan out later when you embrace the blessing that comes from your valley. Instead of trying to understand your walk, trust God to guide your walk. Regardless of how challenging a time in your life may appear, always remember that God will let blessings span from all situations.

Although the steps you are taking now may require you to place your feet upon dry soil, still see the positive light in the situation. The power of the Lord will bless you to lie down in green pastures that flourish with overflowing blessings. God will lead you beside still waters, and the tumultuous tides that you had to overcome will then be a testimony of your journey.

While challenging times may be unfolding in your life today, blessings are still ahead of you when faith lives within your spirit. Never accept the belief that tumultuous tides will always consume your life. The waters ahead of you are not treacherous, nor are they unsteady. They are still. My friend, the stillness reflects the certainty of the outcome of whatever storm is in your life. Certainty of triumph is what you have when your faith resides in the power of the Lord. When hope lives in your heart that God will bring you through whatever is taking place in your life, the illumination of God's greatness will shine as He brings you through it.

Regardless of how your situation may appear on the surface, you must remain positive. Your walk through the valley is only a temporary point as you travel toward your blessings. The valley of the shadow of death is not the end for you. It is only a place that you are passing through to reach greater heights ahead. You must realize that your time in the valley is only a season in your lifetime, not the end of your journey.

It may appear that the more you do your best, the more things seem to get worse. Despite this, still hold your head high! When you want to be the best, you must strive for the best! Embrace these empowering words: *I am walking **through** the valley. The valley is **not** my final place. Great things are ahead of me **beyond** the valley. This is only a **temporary** point before I reach my blessings.*

Blessings begin with your thoughts. The words that you allow to control your thoughts are some of the strongest forces in your life. By remaining positive, you will experience what is positive. When you embrace words of optimism, you will overpower pessimism. As you allow words of greatness to flood your mind, you will stand strong against life's obstacles.

Life experiences have shown me how a positive mindset feeds faith into the spirit. Experiences in my own life have been clear illustrations to me of how the power of God has unfolded to lead me. To outsiders looking into my life, it may appear as if everything on every day of my life has always been a win for me. Although every day of my life has not been a win, I have learned how to turn my stumbles into setups for my steps ahead. Personal experiences have served as a vital teacher for me when it comes to using where I am to blossom toward where I want to be. There have been times when I have just wanted to hang my head in shame and give up on my goals in life. Nevertheless, having faith the size of a mustard seed poured water over me in places of dryness so that blossoming would take place. With faith, I am continually reminded that experiencing the lows of life allows me to enjoy the highs that God blesses me to have.

Faith, prayer, and a positive mindset have shown me how a mess in one place on the table of life can become a miraculous message at another place on the same table. Although a mess may seem to be a terrible thing, always keep in mind that "mess" is the first part of the word "message." A message is what God is sending you through your situation. No matter what your situation happens to be, He is not simply leaving you alone to handle it alone. God is always with you.

Regardless of any situation that comes about in your life, you must still allow your hope to have substance, despite what you do not see. There are so many times in life when we allow ourselves to be defeated before we even take one step toward a goal. My friend, you must believe you can do it before you do it, no matter what "it" happens to be. Roadblocks of the mind must come down. Hope must reside in your heart so that you will overpower any challenge that comes forth.

Everyone wants to be a champion, but you must start pursuing your goal to be a champion. Starting is not always an easy task, but it is worth it for you to become a champion. *What race are you running? What are you working to achieve? After you have finished taking the last step of your walk through the valley, what will you have accomplished?* Take a moment to pause with me. Close your eyes for the next few moments in order to find an answer within your spirit to these questions. Once you have found the best answer to give, open your eyes. Speak the answers to these questions aloud. Give these answers power. Now that you know what you are pursuing for you to become a champion, I want you to give it your all!

To become a champion, you must wake up with the mentality of a champion. Take your first step out of bed believing that you are a champion. If being a champion to you means being a successful business owner, illustrate a picture of yourself in your mind as a successful business owner. If being a champion to you means being a teacher, paint a picture in your mind as a teacher who touches the lives of students on a daily basis. If being a champion to you means being a lawyer, see yourself in your mind winning a pivotal case in the courtroom that others thought could never be won. If being a champion to you means being a doctor, view yourself in your mind as having performed a life-saving surgery on a patient. Whatever being a champion means to you, see yourself as that champion from the moment you get up in the morning to the time you lie down at night.

One of the strongest ways to steer you toward embracing the mentality of a champion is to spiritually define the person you see in the mirror as a champion. I want you to do something with me. Clear your mind. Now, take the next 20 seconds to do nothing but look at yourself. After looking at yourself, come up with three words that enter your mind that describe what you see when you look at yourself. What are those words? If you do not feel that those words describe a champion, we need to change that. My friend, when you can describe someone of greatness when you look at yourself, you are able to define a champion when you look at yourself. To be a champion, you need to see a champion! As a champion, words need to enter your mind that coincide with describing a champion when you look at yourself. Take time every day to enjoy viewing yourself as a champion.

When you look at yourself, you must see a champion. By seeing a champion when you look at yourself, it is much easier to picture one when times get tough. It generally feels much easier to lie down and go to sleep when you feel assured of the blessings that tomorrow will bring as opposed to when you lack the same certainty. Imagine having to wonder overnight if a test that you took earlier in the day will make or break your years of hard work toward a particular career. When you see yourself as a champion, a spiritual ease will allow you to rest easy, because faith will keep you strong. Picture yourself having to sit in a waiting room wondering about the outcome of a family member's surgery. The time that you are waiting will be a time of mental peace when you have the mindset of a champion, because faith will ensure that confidence resides within you.

As well as seeing ourselves as champions, a significant factor is also used to communicate our views as champions: *words*. A person's life can change using words. Words have tremendous power over our lives. Just as the music you listen to can change the pace of your walk, the words you listen to can change the pace of your walk. At one point, you may have a slow, pessimistic walk with each step you take as you walk through the valley. However, this may be changed to an upbeat, optimistic walk with each step you take as you walk through the valley. Why is this? It is because when we listen to words, we allow them to gain a place in our minds. Whether positive or negative, words influence us.

When words have a place in our minds, it is easier for them to flow from our mouths as we speak. My friend, when we speak any words, we give them power. When we speak greatness over who we are, we speak greatness into existence. On the other hand, when we speak negativity over who we are, we speak negativity into existence. Regardless of what words you speak about who you are, let them flow with positivity. Speak blessings into existence. Take the words that God has written on your tongue, and let those words roll out the path to your blessings. Let your mouth articulate songs of praise instead of words of worry. "Let your speech always be with grace, seasoned with salt, that you may know how you ought to answer each one" (Colossians 4:6 NKJV).

When you wake up in the morning, declare that you see a champion! Throughout the day, speak aloud that you are a champion! When you pray to God, embrace the belief that your prayers will be answered! The best way that I can suggest for you to empower your mindset as a champion and strengthen your relationship with the Lord is by connecting to His Word. This is why I highly encourage everyone to read the Bible.

There is so much to learn and so much to be taught through the Word of God. For me personally, I may sit down for a random period to read the Bible, yet I walk away from that time with so many lessons that I have learned from reading the Bible. As such, I take my lessons learned from the Bible, and I bring forth words of motivation for you as my reader. God has blessed me with my passion to touch the lives of others through writing, and He inspires me to read His Word for my motivation to make that happen.

I cannot say enough about how much the Word of God is a powerful tool. Reading the Bible allows us to see the parallels between His Word and what happens in our lives. What may appear to be a letdown may later reflect itself as a blessing in disguise. Imagine sincerely wanting to have a job that pays a $45,000 salary, only to learn that you were not the person selected for the job. Following this, imagine applying for another job that pays a $65,000 salary. Within days you then learn that you were chosen for this job that pays $20,000 more than the job you originally wanted. You never would have received the higher paying job had things gone your way instead of God's way. As we familiarize ourselves with His Word, we better understand His actions.

My friend, a true connection with the Word of God is a vital part of life. Whether it entails reading one scripture each day or a large segment of scriptures on a regular basis, I highly encourage you to read the Word of God. By knowing His Word, it is easier to gain spiritual comfort. When you have spiritual comfort, you know what you are asking of the Lord, and you become prepared to receive it. Keep in mind that when you ask the Lord to answer your prayers, it is important to know what you are asking God to bring into your life.

By having a true connection with the Word of God, you know what you are asking of our Heavenly Father when you pray. Many people ask the Lord to grant them patience without a second thought of what they are asking. Nevertheless, they do not realize what they are asking Him to bring into their lives. "And not only so, but we glory in tribulations also: knowing that tribulation worketh patience" (Romans 5:3 KJV). To gain patience, you must go through trials and tribulations in your life. Be careful what you ask the Lord to bring to you when you kneel before Him in prayer and be ready to receive it.

Having patience is a very important aspect of life. However, we must be prepared for the power of God to move in our lives when we ask for an answer to a prayer, especially one like receiving patience. When we ask for patience, we must be ready for what God will bring into our lives so that we will have it. When we have patience, we have what it takes to wait for our blessings. My friend, with patience within your spirit, you have more than just what it takes to wait. You also have a sense of endurance within yourself that will make you keep going despite the challenges that you may face while you wait. "Be silent before the LORD and wait expectantly for him" (Psalm 37:7 CSB).

Day after day it may appear as if the more effort you put forth to overcome an obstacle, the harder things become. Knowing this, endurance is a significant spiritual ingredient to the foundation of faith. Having the ability to withstand tough challenges that do their best to hold you back from achieving your goals is a key point of what makes or breaks you when it comes to triumph. Waiting on the Lord and showing endurance as He brings you toward your blessings is crucially important to what it takes to keep the faith. "Patient endurance is what you need now, so that you will continue to do God's will. Then you will receive all that He has promised" (Hebrews 10:36 NLT).

Gaining a connection to the Word of God allows us to strengthen our connection to God. By having this, we know that God is always behind us. There are times in life when we may want to hold our heads down in defeat and give up because we do not realize that God is behind us, and He is preparing blessings in front of us. This is when spiritual direction becomes an important element of life. Your focus must not be on points of life that are behind you, but on those that are in front of you. Greatness of all magnitudes may be awaiting you, but you must allow God to do His work. No matter how badly things in the past may appear, looking forward is necessary, not looking backward. My friend, do not live in the past. Grow from the past.

Times will come about in life when God will take you where you need to be before you even realize you are there. This is a significant reason why it is important to look forward in life, not backward. What has happened in the days behind you may seem like letdown after letdown from our Heavenly Father. However, we must remember that He sits high and looks low, and He watches over us as His children during every second of the day.

Points tend to exist in life when we have an idea of where we should be going, but we need God to shift our direction for us to reach our destination. Although the shift that God has brought on your path may appear to be a letdown because of its extra stretch, rest assured that God has the best path planned for you to follow. The steps you are taking today may seem to be too much to handle but keep the faith that you are taking them for a reason.

Despite having already learned a lesson from a situation, God may present a similar situation in our lives to teach us a different lesson. One situation may have the question **What If?** constantly running through our minds. Even so, God presenting a similar situation in our lives may be His way of replacing the question **What If?** with the question **What's Next?**

Situations in life that do not turn out in our favor may have questions of an uncertain nature constantly running through our minds. On a consistent basis, we may have our minds flooded with questions of this likeness: *What if I had started my own company?*

What if I had pursued getting my education? What if I had taken the test when I first thought my health was getting bad? What if I had taken my relationship seriously?

God's work in action often takes us down similar paths that we have previously pursued so that we now have a new question and those of its likeness in our minds: **What's next?** Watch what happens when the questions change from pessimism to optimism because of a slight change of words that take place because of life's lessons: *What's next for my very own company? What's next now that I am pursuing my education? What's next now that I took the test, and the doctor was able to treat my medical condition before it got out of hand? What's next for the great things in my relationship?* All it took was a new approach to following the same path for the words in the questions to change the meanings of the questions completely. My friend, keep in mind that new lessons coming from a previous path tend to be great ways to steer us toward optimism. With optimism comes the ability to take leaps of faith in life that will allow you to rise toward greatness that you never thought you would achieve.

When you can take a leap of faith in life, confidence exists behind the hope that lives within you. With faith, the hope inside of you rests upon assurance that the hand of God will move in your favor. Time is a precious gift from God. It should not be unnecessarily thrown away. When we allow our trust in the Lord to guide us rather than have to worry about the unknown to sway us, we will see spiritual growth take place. Your time in the valley is a time of growth. It is a time of maturity. It is a time that strengthens you. It is a time that leads you on a voyage to the mountaintop of triumph.

Although we cannot physically see our triumphs before they happen, faith makes us hold strong to the confidence that our triumphs will occur. With this, God brings rest to a restless soul. He makes a restless mind become a restful mind. By having rest within us, we can see greatness as we look through faith. "So we fix our eyes not on what is seen, but on what is unseen, since what is seen is temporary, but what is unseen is eternal" (2 Corinthians 4:18 NIV).

Faith and time can be best friends or worst enemies. This tends to be because some individuals can hold on to hope as they trust in the Lord, while others lack hope and do not give God the trust that He deserves. Think of one successful celebrity whose style of entertainment you like. Do you think this person has always been successful? What do you think this person has had to overcome? Why do you think this person overcame his or her challenges?

Even when it takes long periods, time is a smooth factor in the lives of some individuals, yet it is very hard in the lives of others. Some people have an inability to delay gratification. They feel that they must be rewarded *now*! Waiting is not an option, and the word *wait* is not in their vocabulary. This is why they settle for mediocrity in the here and now when they could glow with greatness if they would simply wait. "But they that wait upon the LORD shall renew their strength; they shall mount up with wings as eagles; they shall run, and not be weary; and they shall walk, and not faint" (Isaiah 40:31 KJV).

My friend, do not settle for one thing on your path in life merely because another will require you to wait. When you wait for the hand of God to move in your favor, you can see blessings far beyond your expectations. Do not simply reach your limits. Surpass your limits! Be relentless! Be encouraged! Finish with faith!

Aside from time, past failures are often an aspect of life that hinders a person's desire to move forward instead of remaining where they are. Do not let the failures behind you stand in the way of the victories ahead of you. God teaches you to move beyond failures and appreciate small victories as you walk through the valley. In doing so, you will appreciate the large victories at the end of your valley. No matter how dark the sky may appear over your life, there will still be small victories to appreciate. When you show appreciation for the small victories in your life, you are showing God that you have what it takes for Him to bless you with large victories.

Speak victory over your life! Embrace the mentality that you will take a voyage beyond the valley! Declare the words, "Greatness shall follow me all the days of my life!" Proclaim the words, "Mercy shall follow me all the days of my life!" State the words, "No valley will stop me!" When you speak greatness into existence, greatness will follow you.

God will not bring you to the valley just to leave you there. When things look impossible, faith is the common element to walk through the valley to reach your goal. God is not just the God of green pastures. He is also the God who leads you on your walk through the valley of the shadow of death. The darkness of your valley may seem to be too much to overcome. However, do not use the natural eye to view your valley. Having faith allows you to see the path to follow as you walk through the valley. With this, you know that bad points happening now will not always remain in your life.

This very second may seem like the darkest moment that you have ever endured in your life. It may appear to be the gloomiest midnight hour that you have had to walk through. Keep in mind that after every midnight hour in life, there is still a bright, new morning for you to live. Regardless of how bad things seem to appear, today is still a blessed day. All it takes is faith the size of a mustard seed for you to look at your situation through the eyes of faith so that you can see blessings even on a bad day. My friend, a blessed day is a beautiful day that you can see only with faith.

Just keep this in mind. As I am writing these words for you to read, the Lord is making a way for you and me to solve the problems that we are enduring. Despite what you are going through, hold strong to the belief that God will make a way for you! Keep the faith that regardless of the challenges that exist in your life, there is no challenge that is too hard for God to solve! Of all the wisdom that you may get in life, gaining the wisdom that God will bless you with to overcome your challenges is the best manner of wisdom for you to have. With your wisdom, also look to God for understanding. Although you will not understand all of His ways, you will understand what God desires for you to understand. "Wisdom is the principal thing; therefore, get wisdom: and with all thy getting get understanding" (Proverbs 4:7 KJV).

Having gained the gift of wisdom from the Lord, we are able to appreciate all the days of our lives. With wisdom within us, we will listen to what the Lord has to say to us. My friend, when God speaks to you to do something, you must spiritually get up and do it. One of the most common things that God speaks to us to do is to persevere in the best of times and the worst of times. Perseverance through life's trials is the subtle, yet intense aspect of our lives that separates the winners from those whose definition of a winner always has the word *almost* going along with it. Think of someone who *almost* became a business owner. Reflect upon someone who *almost* became a nurse. Let your mind see someone who *almost* became a lawyer. What do people like these have in common? Each one of them *almost* accomplished a goal, but they did *not* accomplish that goal.

Like perseverance on hard days and easy days, so is the faith of our lives. It only takes faith the size of a mustard seed to make great things happen. This drives our perseverance when faith resides within our spirits. Never forget that faith is what gives you the strength that it takes to persevere, even when you are in life's most difficult times. With faith in the Lord to do great things in your life, you will have what it takes to move beyond limited to limitless. God steps up to challenges when others around us step aside. God will lead you, not merely accompany you. He makes a possibility become reality, as He makes what might happen become what is happening.

Despite the woes that you face as you walk through the valley, always remember that God is in control of every step you take. The steps that you take as you walk through the valley are preparing you to achieve victory. This allows you to open your eyes to excellence when you keep the faith. When you are prepared, being able to look through the eyes of faith becomes an easier task, regardless of where you happen to be in the valley.

One issue that God addresses with our steps in the valley is our location. You may think that you have gone somewhere for one reason only to find out that it is for something entirely different. Looking at where you happen to be through the eyes of man may make you feel as if it is just time to give up. Nevertheless, looking at the same location through the eyes of faith will show you that God took you there to rise to a level that you may have never believed you would reach.

Imagine a man who currently rents an apartment sitting in the office of a bank awaiting the outcome of a home loan application that he believes is the determining factor of buying a home. Moments later, he learns that his home loan application was denied. As he walks out of the bank, it would appear as if he wasted his time even placing his name on the home loan application. Picture someone a short distance away being able to overhear his dissatisfaction with his home loan application being denied. Now, imagine this person stopping him in the parking lot to inquire if he would be interested in taking over the last few monthly payments of a family member's home that is no longer needed, and then having it for himself. With this, he would not need a 30-year home loan from the bank, and all the financial frustrations that would likely go along with it.

Months later, he would then pay off his home, as opposed to having waited 30 years for the final payment of his home. Looking at the bank's location through the eyes of your fellow man in this situation, it was a failure when it came to the home loan application. However, looking at the location through the eyes of faith, it was a testimony of God's greatness. "For the eyes of the Lord are over the righteous, and his ears are open unto their prayers: but the face of the Lord is against them that do evil" (1 Peter 3:12 KJV).

Being knowledgeable of a situation like this certainly speaks of what faith can do. A person in this set of circumstances would have had faith the size of a mustard seed regarding acquiring a home to even walk in the bank. Although things did not turn out the way this man thought they would, the outcome brought forth a much more financially favorable location. The home would now not only be a blessing for him, but also for other generations to come in his family.

The mere faith that he needed in order to step inside the bank paved the way for him to achieve this. This set him apart from many others who would not pursue obtaining a home due to being told by others that failure would be the only outcome of the home pursuit. Before walking out of the bank, this man had a pause in his life when it came to receiving the blessing of his new home. Many people dislike a pause in life, and they do not know how to handle it. Nevertheless, when God brings about a pause, He does so for a reason. When God puts a pause on your path, be thankful for the pause. A pause in your steps is often God's way of adjusting your spiritual lens. This gentleman had a pause between receiving the blessing of a new home from the point of being told that his home loan application was denied to the point of being offered a home that did not need a 30-year home loan. The pause here was certainly something that shows God's work in action.

Although the gentleman walked on the same road that life presented to him as he walked into the bank, he was able to see that same road from a much different angle when he walked out of the bank. He viewed the ability to get a new home from one direction when he walked into the bank, but the way he viewed it was much different when he walked out of the bank. Going into the bank, the gentleman saw the possibility of getting a new home being all in the hands of the application's outcome. Coming out of the bank, he saw the reality of getting a new home resulting from something that a total stranger was willing to provide. My friend, the same road may look different when you are traveling in a different direction. Keep in mind that God will sometimes shift the way you are walking through the valley so that you can see a much better direction in which to walk.

Your walk through the valley prepares you for the blessings ahead of you. Just as the previous gentleman had a hunger to move beyond an apartment and into a home, there is something for which you hunger to have. My friend, God gives us an appetite for prosperity, not failure. He provides us with an appetite for our blessings. Our Heavenly Father puts substance behind what we hope to have in life. Keep in mind that worry closes the eyes of faith, but hope opens the eyes of faith. When we look at the situations in our lives through the eyes of faith, we can see that faith moves doubt aside. With faith, doubt will be something in our lives that lessens. God brings us toward faith so that we will embrace it and rise above the low points in our lives.

The spiritual audacity of faith gives you the courage not only to take the first step into the valley but to walk through the valley. Your focus should not rest on preparing for your walk through the valley. It should be on using your walk through the valley to empower you to reach greater heights. My friend, you have the spiritual audacity to have faith because you know there is power in the name of Jesus, regardless of your situation. From the rising of the sun, the Lord has great things planned for you. To the setting of the sun, the Lord has great things planned for you. Let this belief resonate throughout your spirit on the best of days and the worst of days.

Too many times in life we allow ourselves to be led by what man has to say. Nevertheless, we often have a lack of understanding with this. We must keep in mind that when man speaks, things may or may not happen. On the other hand, things always happen when God speaks. The favor of man is limited, but the favor of God is unlimited. There are often points in life when things do not happen the way we want them to happen. This is why we are often willing to go along with what man has to say, although it is not in correlation with our goals.

Your right time is set at a place on God's calendar. You must realize that the moment God places a dream in your heart, He has already placed the right time for it to happen on His calendar. We often want things to go ahead and happen because it seems too hard to wait for what we want to take place in our lives. Keep in mind that rushing things along moves us on a different path as opposed to what takes place when we follow God's timing.

My friend, just as the right time exists, the wrong time also exists. God prepares us to receive our blessings before He places them in our lives. By doing this, He ensures that we are ready to have them in our lives. Although we may not receive our blessings on our timetable, we must keep the faith in order to receive them. Declare these words in your mind, let them rest in your heart, and embrace them in your spirit: *I did not come this far just to come to this very place as my stopping point! I have more steps to take! I will be blessed!*

Being able to blossom with our blessings spiritually requires us to believe in our hearts that nothing and no one can overpower God when it comes to being blessed with what He has for us. If it is in God's plan, nothing and no one will undo it. In the best of times and the worst of times, keep the faith that you will receive God's favor. My friend, keep the faith as you rise beyond heights that you never imagined. On the same token, keep the faith during what appears to be a fall, no matter how big or small. "For the LORD Almighty has purposed, and who can thwart him? His hand is stretched out, and who can turn it back?" (Isaiah 14:27 NIV).

With the steps you take as you walk through the valley, stop yourself from simply going through the motions. Reflect upon why you are even in the valley that God is taking you through. Take the time to see that no matter how bad your valley seems, each step you take is guided by the Lord. Let faith be the shoes in which you walk, not sight. By having these things in mind, a needed change to how you walk through the valley will take place. Changing your approach tends to be what is needed to get the different results that God is leading you toward so that you will receive your blessings. My friend, walk worthy according to where God orders your steps.

New thoughts lead the way to new behaviors. New behaviors lead the way to new outcomes. Taking a new approach in life often allows us to see the strength of God's power. There are times in life when your fellow man will speak so much negativity toward you to bring you down that a new approach on your part will be needed. Although your fellow man may speak negative words over and over, all it takes is for God to speak one word to override this. A situation that mirrored this was when a gentleman had his temporary supervisor constantly coming to him with nothing but negativity to express. It began to appear to him that his efforts were not worth anything in the eyes of the temporary supervisor, and the job was not worth him putting his time toward doing.

At the point when he began to feel that he was reaching his breaking point, God spoke one word: *SNOW*! With this, massive shutdowns of businesses throughout his area occurred for multiple days. Temperatures went from being at record highs on one day to being in freezing temperatures on the next day. As such, the gentleman had the next few days to evaluate his situation. He was able to gain insight into how he could leave his toxic work environment and use his knowledge and skills to rise higher in life.

Although his temporary supervisor spoke *many* words in continuous attempts to tear him down, it took only *one* word for God to speak in order to guide the gentleman toward a much better place. When he was gone, the temporary supervisor realized what was significantly lacking without the gentleman, but it was too late to bring him back. Upon the main supervisor's return, things were at a much lower performance. Some of the gentleman's former coworkers informed the main supervisor of the temporary supervisor's mistreatment of the gentleman, and how that was likely the driving force that led him to leave. With this, the main supervisor contacted the gentleman attempting to get him to return. However, he clearly made it known that he had no interest in returning.

Day after day, the gentleman previously attempted to see what he was doing wrong to make the temporary supervisor dislike him so much. Nonetheless, it was not what he was doing wrong that was the issue. It was God showing him that it was time for a change. We must remember that sometimes what we are looking for is right in front of us, which is why it is very important for us to see things from the proper perspective. On the days when the gentleman was not able to leave his home due to the weather conditions, he was able to take a step back and see things from the proper perspective. God shifted the steps he was taking to a different direction that was a better direction for him. My friend, it is not about the valley that you walk through. It is where God leads you that counts. Always look to the Lord for guidance, because He is using the valley as a tool to bring you to a better place.

Being able to blossom with blessings in our lives is something that we all want. However, we must be willing to take the steps that will lead us to those blessings. Taking steps through the valley can be so challenging that we get to a place that makes us want to just throw in the towel and turn around on our blessings. It could be that you are struggling to keep your incredibly talented child on the proper course in life, but it appears that there is nothing else you can do to help the situation. On one hand, you could simply let the situation go and let the chips fall where they may. On the other hand, you could let go and let God control the situation. By holding onto faith in your spirit, you can see that there is no situation that is too hard for God to handle.

How do *you* walk as you take steps through the valley? Do you walk with hesitation in your situation, or do you walk with confidence that the Lord will work things out? You may not be able to control the valley, but you can control how you walk through the valley. When the steps you take are guided by worry, doubt, and pessimism, you will be led toward limitations and persuaded to give in to failure. At the same time, when the steps you take are guided by hope and faith, you will be led toward the blessings that God has waiting to blossom in your life.

Hope can be the product of life's biggest disasters, and faith can serve as the key to trade your disasters for triumphs. A disaster may lead to the question, "How can I get out of this?" However, having faith within the disaster leads to the statement, "I *will* overcome this!" You cannot allow life's occurrences to overpower your faith. No matter how big or small a challenge in life happens to be, always hold strong to the belief that God will see you through it.

There are times in life when we allow small situations to overtake our attention, which leads to periods when we give those times the power to lessen our faith. Imagine being at work around colleagues who begin to communicate in a fashion that you do not understand whenever you approach them, or they begin to physically distance themselves when they see you coming. Giving power to such situations allows you to question your faith because doubt and worry begin to become leading factors in your life. Nevertheless, if these were individuals who God meant to be strong people in your life, He would not have them doing such small things. My friend, do not give power to small things when God has great things ahead of you.

Keep in mind that you are a valuable child of our Heavenly Father, and time is one of the most valuable things that He has given you. By giving your valuable gift of time to small things and small situations, you give those small things and small situations the large key to your mind. You allow those small things and small situations to mold and shape who you are as a person, which drives you in an improper direction in life.

Have you ever been away from a negative person or undesirable situation, but still had that same negative person or undesirable situation on your mind throughout large portions of your day? *Why is that?* It is because you are giving it the key to your mind. You are giving it power over who you are. When you give something your time, you give it power. When you give someone your time, you give that person power. Do not give your time away so easily, especially not to people or situations that thrive upon negativity in your life.

In the last seven days, has there been something that you have noticed that you are dwelling upon more than you should? By doing this, you are allowing your time to be limited to what you are dwelling upon. The more you allow this to happen, the more you allow it to have control over you. Do not let something negative have control over you. Take control of your time. Spending time wishing something did not happen gives it power over you. My friend, accept it as a part of your past and move forward with your life.

You must have a selective spirit when it comes to what you allow to have your time, not a careless spirit. Do not give the key to your time to anything and everything that wants it. Do not give your time to anyone who wants it. The next time you notice that something or someone negative is constantly overtaking your thoughts, make a vow to yourself that you will stop allowing this to happen. Make a vow to take back your time. When you do this, you will not constantly give negative things or negative people the key to one of the most important gifts that you have: *time*. My friend, you cannot control every second of your life, but you can control who and what you easily let have your time.

One of the strongest ways that we can retain control of our time is by recognizing our expectancy. As you walk through the valley, where you expect to finish will serve as a strong map that leads to where you will finish. Do you expect to finish at a lower place than where you were before you first stepped into the valley? Do you expect to finish at the same place where you were before you first stepped into the valley? On the other hand, do you expect to finish at a much higher place than where you were before you first stepped into the valley?

By shifting what you expect toward greater things, you allow your time to focus on greater expectations. Your actions will center around greater expectations, and your faith will heighten your works to allow blessings to blossom in your life by the hand of God. No matter how things may seem at this very moment, always keep in mind that our Heavenly Father guides each moment of our lives. Our faith in God will overshadow every seemingly impossible challenge that we may face and anything that may be done to bring us down.

Do not pollute your spirit with doubt and worry. Let faith steer you forward, and let spiritual restlessness lose its place in your life. Look up to the Lord with confidence, not down with doubt. Instead of contaminating yourself with frustration, freshen yourself with faith. Instead of allowing your faith to be watered down by bad experiences of your past, let it be enhanced by the expectations of great experiences ahead of you.

As you are in the very place where you are at this moment, you may be worrying about how you will overcome a setback in your life that no one else knows you are facing. My friend, I want you to stop worrying about possible bad things and start expecting great things. Think about the last time God brought you out of a setback in your life. What took place? Why didn't you fail instead of rising above the setback? How did that become a testimony in your life instead of a loss that you could not move beyond? The same quality of answers that you can provide for these questions sets forth the same quality of reasons why faith should reside in your spirit, not worry.

Do not embrace spiritual poverty. Embrace spiritual surplus. Look at what is happening in your life like a math problem that you must answer. Before you find the correct answer, you must first work on the problem. The same reasoning applies here. Before you step out of the valley with the correct answer, you must first work on the problem by walking through the valley. Stepping out of the valley comes with an answer from the Lord after you have done your work.

Just as we have our own obstacles to endure, Jesus Christ Himself had His own obstacles to endure. He had His own valley to walk through prior to His blessing of resurrection. Jesus was pierced for our sins during His time as He walked through His own valley for our benefit. This serves as a reminder that we as His followers must know that although there will be times when we will endure pain and suffering, we will have much brighter days ahead when we keep the faith. We must further keep in mind that the ache and sorrow that Jesus Christ underwent was for us. "But he was wounded for our transgressions, he was bruised for our iniquities: the chastisement of our peace was upon him; and with his stripes we are healed" (Isaiah 53:5 KJV).

No matter what is happening in your life, never forget that no situation is too much for the Lord. Jesus Christ Himself rose from the pain and suffering that He had to endure on behalf of His followers. Death was not enough for Him. "He is not here; he has risen, just as he said. Come and see the place where he lay" (Matthew 28:6 NIV).

We should show thankfulness to Jesus as we walk through the valley. With each step you take, never forget the burdens that Jesus carried before He rose with all the power of Heaven and Earth in His hands. Knowing this, we should keep in mind that there is no step that we must take in life that He cannot properly place when we keep the faith. Jesus Christ will lead you through any crisis that you may face in life. With faith in your spirit, you will walk through the valley and not be overwhelmed by the obstacles that confront you.

Obstacles tend to engulf our minds without us even realizing it. My friend, it takes spiritual maturity to enjoy what is happening now instead of allowing the future to drain your focus. Allowing the future to consume our minds is often the biggest reason we allow challenges to feed into our worries, which keeps them alive. Nevertheless, we must remember that the Lord has compassion for every step we take. While obstacles in life may appear to be too much to walk beyond, our trust in the Lord gives us the strength that we need to step over our obstacles. As we hold strong to the faith that we need to step over our obstacles, we gain spiritual maturity.

The ground is not soft and smooth as you walk through the valley. It is rough and rugged. There may be thorns that pierce your spiritual feet, and situations that seem harmful to your spirit. Although we are walking through a valley as we endure challenging times, the ground upon which we walk is laid with mercy from the Lord. With this in mind, we can spiritually grasp the idea that no step that we take is too much for God to properly place on our path as we walk toward our blessings. "It is of the LORD's mercies that we are not consumed, because his compassions fail not. They are new every morning: great is thy faithfulness" (Lamentations 3:22-23 KJV).

Your time in the valley is not meant to stop you, but to prepare you for greater things ahead. Do not see your challenges during hard times as failures, but as lessons that serve as moments to mold you. The Lord will bring you through what you are having to endure with the steps you are taking as you walk through the valley. Trust God for what He can do in your life beyond what you see happening now. Do not let your focus reside upon what may not take place, but trust God for what He will let take place. Although you must walk through the valley before you will see your blessings blossom, keep in mind that God is writing a new chapter of your life with those blessings. He will bring you through what you are having to endure.

There will be days when it may seem as if the steps you are taking as you walk through the valley are totally off track. It may appear as if you walked well for a long period of time only to have your steps knocked off track. Do not simply see the negativity in such a situation. Remember there are times when you must take a step back so that you can see where you are now. What is God telling you by having you step back? What is it that you can see about where you are now that makes you see where you need to be in the future? My friend, always pay attention to what God is doing with where He places you.

What challenges are you facing as you walk through the valley? Why do you think God is allowing those challenges into your life? Never forget that nothing takes place in your life without God first ordaining it to happen. He is the author of each page of your life. Instead of living with frustration and complaining about the challenges that God has placed before you, look to the Lord to find out why He has placed the challenges before you.

Keep in mind that in order to walk through the valley, you must confront your challenges. There is no challenge that stands in front of you that you cannot overcome when the will of God combines with your faith in His power. If your challenge was too much for God to handle, then I could understand even the smallest level of worry that you would have about your challenge. Nevertheless, *nothing* is too much for God! If God means for your challenge to be brought down, all it takes from you is faith the size of a mustard seed for you to see today's challenge become tomorrow's testimony. Do not see your obstacles as downfalls but as opportunities to blossom!

Always keep in mind that each step you take as you walk through the valley is a part of God's plan for your life. So many people see where they are at this very moment and where they want to be, but they do not have a plan to follow for how to get there. Just like a gardener must have a plan for how to make flowers blossom, you must have a plan for how you will make your blessings blossom. You cannot just wake up in the morning one day and say, "God I want a new house." If that new house is the blessing that you want from God, you must look to Him for a plan to get it. Pray to the Lord for guidance. Look to Him for direction. Let God's plan enter your spirit and direct your thoughts. Put preparation in the place of fear.

Behind every action exists a plan. The plan of action that you take will lead you toward your goal. When you act, you open the door for opportunities to come into your life. Let the adversities that you are enduring today become the opportunities that you will take advantage of tomorrow. Some people overlook opportunities that are presented to them because they feel they are too small. However, what is small today will become big in its time. No matter how small a current opportunity may seem, take the time to consider it. The opportunity may be something that will help you grow. Always keep in mind that you do not want to overlook what could be used to allow you to rise toward greater heights.

What is the blessing that you want to receive from God? My friend, I want you to gain a spiritual attachment to the blessing that you want to receive from God. Stand in front of your mirror every morning and speak the words of your blessing aloud. Speak your blessing into existence. When you get ready to go to bed, stand in front of your mirror and speak the words of your blessing aloud. Keep the faith that God will make your blessing blossom in your life!

There have been so many times when I have heard countless people use the word *can* when referring to their goals. "I *can* be successful. I *can* be blessed. I *can* reach my goals." If *can* is a leading word in your spiritual vocabulary, I want you to take the time to adjust your spiritual vocabulary. Take the word *can* out and replace it with the word *will*. "I *will* be successful. I *will* be blessed. I *will* reach my goals." When you have the belief within your spirit that you *will* be blessed, you embrace the blessings that God has in store for you.

Faith is your vehicle to your blessings, and your plan is how you drive it. Look to God for your plan. Pray to our Heavenly Father for your plan. Too often people stop pursuing their plans to reach their goals because they do not see the results that they want in the time frame that they want. However, that is not how you will spiritually blossom. Think of a farmer who makes money after he sells his crops once they blossom. He would certainly want his crops to blossom in an immediate time frame, but that is not how it takes place. Just as he must wait for his crops to blossom, you must wait for your blessings to blossom. My friend, you cannot have an inability to delay gratification if you want to be blessed. You must wait for the

Lord to work in your life so that you will see His greatness through your blessings.

If you did not walk through the valley, you would not have a mountaintop on which you could stand. Your time in the valley may seem rough but remember that it is a time of God's will in practice. It is a place where God has designed for you to grow. The valley is not a place where those who are against you will overpower you. It is a place where the hand of God will move you to greater heights with the increase of your blessings. By trusting God to guide your steps, you will see your blessings materialize.

One point of life tends to be a strong entity that hinders us from reaching our blessings: *the past*. Times exist when we either do not want to confront the past, or we spend too much time focusing upon the past. My friend, always remember that prayer is a guiding aspect of life that takes away the twists and turns of timing, and it brings trust of the Lord within your spirit. Praying to our Heavenly Father and trusting His works allows us to be at peace with the past, embrace the present, and prepare for the future.

When you trust God to control what has happened in your past, the worry and doubt that exist within you will come to rest. You must know what is behind you so that you will be prepared for what is in front of you. My friend, do not forget the past. Grow from the past. However, remember that the past is just that…the past. It has already taken place, and it is not meant to take place now.

The present is what is happening now. It is what is on God's schedule to take place now. Your future has not yet happened, and it is not scheduled to have happened. God's timing is the right timing. Trust the plans that God has for you. Know that He will bless you. Keep the faith that the blessings that He has prepared for you are awaiting you.

Think confidently about your blessings. Commit faithfully to your blessings. Focus spiritually upon your blessings. Let hope serve as spiritual water to quench the thirst of your blessings. Keep the faith that your blessings will blossom. After you walk through the valley, God does not mean for you to go back to where you were before. The Lord will place you at a higher standpoint, and you will reign over the troubles of your past. Declare these words to yourself: *I will have my victory over the valley! Blessings will blossom in my life!*

Chapter Four

WALKING WITH FAITHFUL STEPS

Purpose. **Reason.** **Destiny.** These three words are among millions of others enclosed within the pages of a dictionary, yet the power that they have stands out among any set of words where they are placed. When you know your **purpose** on a path, there is a **reason** behind every step you take. Your steps lead to your **destiny**. My friend, understand this if you understand nothing else. Every step that you take has a purpose behind it. Knowing this, boldly take steps in life with faith, regardless of how your path appears on the surface. Take deliberate steps, not indecisive steps. Although there is a valley for you to walk through before you reach your destiny, let your footsteps powerfully proclaim your movement forward in life.

As you walk through the valley with faith in your spirit, every crooked place is being made straight through the power of the Lord. Every pothole is being filled by His grace. Always remember that when faith lives within your spirit, a stumble in the valley is a setup for you to rise to newer and greater heights. After you walk through the valley, you will have a sense of renewal. A spiritual focus will live inside of you. Focus is one of the most powerful elements for your spirit to have. A lack of focus will make you fall, but the presence of focus will bless you to rise.

Too often our focus is not where it needs to be. Yesterday has happened. Today is happening. Tomorrow will happen. You cannot change what has already happened. Even so, you can change what is happening, and this will lead toward what will happen. It takes placing your focus upon the right place in your life to reach greater heights.

Remaining focused in life can serve as a significant challenge. It is easy to stand tall when you are at a peak in life. However, you must also be able to stand tall as you walk through the valley. When faced with setbacks in life, coming up with a plan to overcome the setbacks tends to be one of the last things on our minds. Nevertheless, it should be one of the first things on our minds. Our focus on victory is so easily brushed aside during hard times. In the midst of hard times, questions of this nature often manifest in our minds: *Why isn't there sunshine over every day of my life? Why is there even one second of rain?* Although we may not understand why, the troubles that are raining down upon us have reasons for their presence.

Do you ever feel like you are taking normal steps in life at one moment only to be thrown into a walk through the valley of the shadow of death in the next moment? What makes you feel that way? My friend, when we take our spiritual eyes off our trust in God, we allow doubt to bring about a fog that blurs our beliefs. Trusting God tends to be an easy task during the brightness of high noon. However, it tends to be a challenging obstacle in the darkness of the midnight hour. Despite this, God must be able to see that we trust Him with very little before He will bless us with very much. "Whoever can be trusted with very little can also be trusted with much, and whoever is dishonest with very little will also be dishonest with much" (Luke 16:10 NIV).

Trusting God takes very little effort when things are happening in our favor. When we receive promotions at companies where we have worked for many years, our test results show that we do not have a disease that is difficult to treat, or when we find the love of our lives, trusting God is an easy task. On the other hand, trusting God may appear to be much more challenging when we have been laid off from a company where we have worked for many years, our test results show that we have a disease that is difficult to treat, or when finding love appears to be something that will never happen for us. Taking footsteps forward as you walk through the valley may seem to present new challenges with each step you take. However, you must always remember that you are never alone. With each step you take, God is right there with you.

Despite the troubles that are present in your life, you are *not* by yourself. My friend, you are *not* alone. Our Heavenly Father is walking with you with each step you take in every moment of your life. There is no step that you will take alone as you walk through the valley of the shadow of death. Times in life may come about when it appears to be too hard to take one more step in life, because it feels like there is nothing more that you are able to do. Nevertheless, always hold onto the belief that God is right there with you, regardless how your situation appears.

The trust that you have in God transfers to your belief in His power to move in your life. Your belief is what drives your faith, and your faith is what brings you to victory. By trusting God, you open yourself up to receive the works of His power in your life. We all believe in something. Whether your belief is in victory or defeat, your belief resides in one or the other. Instead of having your belief waver in the face of uncertainty, let your trust in the Lord overpower the doubt that may exist inside you.

Things that are easy on one day tend to become difficult on another day. Not being able to climb one hill at a particular time tends to teach and empower you to climb and stand tall on an even better one. Often when we try to settle for less than what we should have, God will take us through more challenging times of life so that we will aim higher. We must recognize that God wants us to be blessed despite our challenges. My friend, please understand that positive points live even within the word "no." If "yes" allowed a lesser door to open, you would not walk through the better door, and this would not serve as a blessing for you. Do not let "no" reflect upon your value. Let "no" teach you a lesson. God has greatness waiting for you even in the midst of your obstacles. Through all the bumps and bruises that we may encounter in life, the Lord has bandages that will heal them.

God has aligned every point of your life with a reason behind it. The right people have already been aligned where they need to be in your life. The right opportunities have already been aligned at the points where they need to be. The right moment of victory has already been aligned for you to receive it. No matter how difficult your days may seem, make it a habit to repeat these words: *I will not give up! I am walking through this point of my life, not staying here! I will reach my destination!*

You will not permanently live in times of difficulty. These points in your life are only temporary. Do not allow yourself to be blinded by negativity and pessimism. Reflect upon what precipitated pessimistic thoughts in your mind. Then, go to the Lord in prayer to remove this problem. Let your focus be on peace, not problems. My friend, God does not make your mind unconditionally surrender to your problems in order for you to have peace. When you trust in God, faith calms your spirit and grants you peace of mind.

No matter what your situation happens to be, keep the faith! Look at your situation through the eyes of faith, not the eyes of man. Faith overshadows your physical eyes with your spiritual eyes, because it makes you see beneath the limited vision of man. As faith resides within your spirit, your current situation becomes a motivation toward better times ahead. Knowing this, the belief that better days will come takes away your worries associated with yesterday, today, and the days ahead of you. Worry wonders if things will happen, but faith makes things happen.

With belief in your heart, let faith be the driving force of your spirit. Press on because your walk through the valley is not permanent. It is only temporary. God will take your situation from temporary setbacks to triumphant victories. He will make the anxieties of this very moment become the points of peace in the moments to come. Just keep the faith! "Cast all your anxiety on him because he cares for you" (1 Peter 5:7 NIV).

Your walk through the valley is about your obedience to God. Your time in the valley is a time of testing. He is testing the strength that you have within yourself to step out on faith and receive His favor. Do not believe that God does not have a blessing waiting for you because things are not unfolding the way you originally wanted. For every call you make that is not answered, there is a reason. For every call you miss, there is a reason. For every piece of mail that does not come to you, there is a reason. It takes learning to be faithful to the Lord in the worst of times in order to be faithful to Him in the best of times.

God makes it known through His actions that He is more than willing to lead you to your blessings. However, for that to take place,

He must first order your steps as you walk through the valley. In doing so, you must show Him that you can handle walking through low points in life before He will let you stand on the high points. The same God who blesses you amid green pastures is the same God who blesses you amid a walk through the valley. Just keep the faith!

What is the valley in your life? Addictions? Unemployment? Loneliness? Abuse? Health problems? Loss of a loved one? Financial setbacks? For the next 60 seconds, I want you to close your eyes and think of the moment when you first stepped foot in your valley. Reflect upon how your life changed when this took place. Now, open your eyes. What was it like to enter your valley? How were you different after entering your valley than you were before? Do you believe you have what it takes to walk through your valley, or do you believe your valley is a permanent place that you do not have what it takes to walk through? Is there a part of you with faith even the size of a mustard seed to believe that you will rise above your valley and reach a point of victory?

A walk through the valley tends to be one of the last things in life that we expect to happen. It is much different when something happens that we expect to happen, as opposed to something that we do not expect. Imagine being a stellar student who has academically excelled for many years. As a result, you have been selected to receive a full-ride scholarship to a well-respected university. All you must do is continue making grades like those you have made for years. However, you later experience a low-performing semester when your grades drop below the GPA requirement, and you lose your scholarship. At this point, you can no longer afford to be a student at this university. What do you do now?

When roads in your life meet, and a fork comes between them, what do you do? You can lie down to your challenges and accept defeat, or you can hold your head high as you look to the Lord for a solution that will lead you to victory. When you look to the Lord, He steers your vision toward victory. A casual glance toward victory differs significantly from directly staring at it. By staring at victory, you have a clear gaze upon it. As such, you see greatness ahead of you. This creates an openness for faith to do its work within you, and you turn things over to God to work for you. With faith in the Lord to move in your life, you embrace the confidence that nothing and no one will push you aside from the blessings He has for you.

My friend, I cannot emphasize enough the importance of having a relationship with the Lord. When you know the Lord, you embrace faith. You stand taller in the face of a challenge when you have faith. While doubt makes you gravitate toward defeat, faith pulls you toward victory. "Even in darkness light dawns for the upright, for those who are gracious and compassionate and righteous" (Psalm 112:4 NIV).

I once met a woman who told me about her son's past as a star football player. However, due to a drug addiction, he went from a path toward the NFL to being homeless. His mother told me that this kept her up night after night for months on end. She said that the same people who had nothing but positive things to say about her son when they believed he would be drafted to the NFL became the same people who talked down upon him over and over. Nevertheless, he turned his life around. He broke free from drug addiction, re-enrolled in college, and earned a degree. Following this, he became a well-respected corporate executive. Her son walked through his valley of drug addiction and achieved success in the world of business.

Do not let a challenge serve as intimidation, but motivation. Let your challenge remind you of your dependence upon God, not your uncertainty with man. Although there are periods of time when you will walk through the valley of the shadow of death, never forget that our Heavenly Father speaks life over all situations! God has situated your circumstances where they need to be. No matter how difficult the obstacles in your life may appear, still be thankful to God for His works in your life, not thankless. Do not let the past stop you from achieving the greatness that God has for you. You can't change the past, so let the sun rise and set with no regrets about what has occurred. Step forward with God's guidance, not backward with direction from man.

Your walk through the valley is a time that empowers your spirit. Every second of the day serves as a time when God can empower you by setting the stage for tests in your life to become testimonies of what you have done with your time. It is not the day that matters. What you do with the day is what matters. Your decisions during the day serve as empowering moments. Making a decision with faith at one moment is vastly different from making a decision without faith at the same moment. The faith behind each step that you take in the valley shows that you are not a weak person, but a child of God who is awaiting victory.

The Lord uses the steps we take in the valley to strengthen us. My friend, when a blessing comes about in our lives, it will come in accordance with the will of God. It is important to realize that God brings our blessings to life to allow us to flourish, not to serve as burdens. We must have the strength within ourselves to handle what God will give us. For something to enter our lives as a blessing, it must enter when the time is right for it to happen. Always remember that *delay* and *deny* do not have the same definition. God tends to delay blessings so that they will come at the right time in our lives. "At the right time, I, the LORD, will make it happen" (Isaiah 60:22 NLT).

Although we may want something right now, things could go terribly wrong if God answered our prayers the way we want right now instead of the way He knows is best. Imagine wanting to have an expensive new car that your income does not financially support you to have. Despite the reality that it may be a car that you have wanted for years, your inability to pay your car note could lead to repossession of the car and have highly negative effects on your credit score. On the other hand, if you were to get the car at a time when you have the financial means to pay for it, the car would serve as a blessing, not a burden. Instead of merely wanting something that you are not prepared to have, or settling for what you do not want, prepare yourself for the greatness that God has ahead of you.

Settling for certain things in life can lead us away from our blessings and open the door to burdens in our lives. Millions of people often confuse convenience with a blessing. My friend, the convenient choice is not always the best choice. We often see in life that the convenient choice tends to be synonymous with the mediocre choice. Do not have complacency with mediocrity. If you reach for mediocrity, you will only get mediocrity. Spread your wings more and more each day! Always strive to soar in life! See your cup overflowing with blessings!

Embracing convenience over risk-taking tends to stem from losses in the past. While a person may have suffered only one loss after countless prior wins, the effects of the loss may be rippling. Nevertheless, do not let a past loss cause improper measurements on your barometer of success. Do not look back. Looking back is an unnecessary action that wastes time and energy. Use your time and energy in a much more productive way. Step forward!

Think the *best* of yourself! Look beyond whatever blemishes you may have. Embrace the positive points of who you are. Hear the voice of optimism speaking when your voice is heard. Walk in faith, not fear. Choose faith over fear. "For God has not given us a spirit of fear, but of power and of love and of a sound mind" (2 Timothy 1:7 NKJV).

A spirit of fear is a set of clothing that cannot be worn with shoes of faith. When fear lives within your spirit, taking the footsteps of faith is a nearly impossible task, due to the need to see your blessings here and now. Faith does not co-exist with an inability to delay gratification. While you cannot physically see your future blessings here and now, you can spiritually see them when faith is present within you. Let your faith rise high and your fears fall low.

What is your vision? How do you see this vision? Why do you see this vision? My friend, you must first have a vision for what is ahead of you before you are able to spiritually see it. One of the main ways to invite failure into your life is to not have a vision for where you are going before you set out on your path. Regardless of how dark the moments in your life may happen to be, always see the light ahead.

Having a vision of faith is one of the strongest ways to be led toward our blessings. We may see that although a blessing seems to be too much to gain on our own, nothing is impossible with God. The faith within us coincides with the power of God unleashing upon our lives. Although there will be times when we feel like we have everything under control by ourselves, there will also be times when we see that we directly need God to step in and make something happen if it will ever occur. "My grace is sufficient for thee: for my strength is made perfect in weakness" (2 Corinthians 12:9 KJV).

Your walk through the valley is a humbling experience for you. The piercing that comes into your spiritual footsteps as you walk through the valley removes pride from your spirit and replaces it with humility. There are times in life when individuals will forget where they came from before God moved them to higher places. People will even forget that God is who brought about their blessings. At these points in life, God will often bring about a shift in the valley to replace pride with humility.

As you gain humility, pride is decreased within your spirit. Boastfulness is lessened. Arrogance is removed. Your level of maturity is heightened and strengthened. "For it is by grace you have been saved, through faith—and this is not from yourselves, it is the gift of God—not by works, so that no one can boast" (Ephesians 2:8-9 NIV).

When hard times present themselves in our lives, they are often some of the most difficult things to understand. *Why did my test results come back like this? What did I do to make my marriage end? How did I go from financial success to living from paycheck to paycheck?* Hard times in our lives tend to be tools that God uses to mold our personalities into the fashion that He wants to see them. As hard times make us mature in faith, we become much stronger individuals. Regardless of what hard times you may endure, when strength lives within your spirit, you will gravitate toward greatness.

No matter what is happening in your life, align your faith with your situation. Have hope that your situation will turn in your favor. Believe that great things will come to pass when all is said and done. Be careful how you see your life. Instead of allowing darkness to cloud your vision, let sunlight brighten your view toward better times ahead.

When things appear to be too much for you to bear, stop and ask yourself this question: *Will the sun of a new day rise after my perseverance through hard times, or will it set in the night of my defeat?* If you are doubtful about how to answer this question in a confident manner, stop and pray to the Lord for guidance. Never accept a defeated mentality. Pray to the Lord for an attitude of perseverance. Open your mind to determination.

One of the most powerful things that puts faith within your spiritual walk as you take steps through the valley is guidance from God. Guidance from God is needed to walk beyond the obstacles that man will tell you that you cannot overcome. With guidance from God, you will stand on the mountaintop of triumph after walking through the valley of the shadow of death.

My friend, internalize the belief that no set of circumstances will stop you in life! Passionately pursue your goals with determination in your heart and faith within your spiritual footsteps. Let resilience burst through you! When things are not going your way, make the effort to turn the tables. Intercept the ball in life when it is not coming to you. No matter how much pressure may be on you, use it as a tool to mold and shape yourself for the better.

When it becomes difficult to take your steps through the valley, let these words echo in your mind: *God is my saving grace! He keeps me from being broken!* Always remember that God specializes in every area of life. A doctor may specialize in only one area of medicine and a lawyer may specialize in only one area of law, but God covers all areas. Our Heavenly Father is the most highly requested lawyer for every courtroom and the best doctor for all of His patients!

When faith lives within you, spiritual struggles transform weaknesses into strengths. With faith, thriving times of triumph become the outcome of your worst days. You learn how to cope with stress and rise above challenges. Resilience perpetuates through you. God restores awesomeness within your spirit when you have faith even as small as a mustard seed. "He restoreth my soul: he leadeth me in the paths of righteousness for his name's sake" (Psalm 23:3 KJV).

With awesomeness present again, our spiritual sight is renewed. The way we view what we see tends to stand out to God as something that He must refresh at points in our lives. Things in life appear small when they are far away, but big when they are up close. We may see our blessings as things that are too small when challenges come with them. However, when our view of the blessings God has for us changes, this tends to make us see that our steps toward our blessings are worth taking.

Having the correct spiritual view allows us to choose what is best for us to have. One of the major reasons why many people shy away from moving forward to see their blessings comes from wearing shoes of fear rather than shoes of faith. Selecting the wrong pair of shoes as you walk on your path may bring about significant problems in life because it causes problems with your view.

We are often able to see that it is easy to back up on a straight line, but much harder to move forward at an angle. Imagine yourself backing out of your driveway with ease. Now, picture yourself having to move forward onto a new road that is at an angle of where you currently are, not to mention having to deal with oncoming traffic during your transition. The same logic often parallels with life's happenings as we attempt to move forward. Although it is easy to back up into familiar territory, it tends to be harder to move forward into unfamiliar territory. This is especially true when that unfamiliar territory comes at an angle instead of being on a straight pattern to follow.

Movement in life is one of the strongest factors that brings out the fire within us. As we move forward, we see that one way is not always the only way, nor is it always the best way. When one lane is closed, do not be afraid to move to a different lane. View your movement as a progression, not a regression. Know that what happens along the way as you walk through the valley is preparing you for the rewards of your blessings. Believe in your heart that good things are coming to you, which will serve as rewards to you for following our Heavenly Father. Do not be too afraid to take a risk to get a reward. "Trouble pursues the sinner, but the righteous are rewarded with good things" (Proverbs 13:21 NIV).

Do your actions demonstrate a belief within you that you will walk through the valley of the shadow of death and rise to the mountaintop of triumph? If not, you will naturally gravitate toward an acceptance of defeat. Instead of having footsteps of faith, you will have footsteps of failure. You may have shoes that are the same size, but you cannot wear two different sets at the same time. If you wear shoes of failure, you will walk into failure. Nevertheless, if you wear shoes of faith, you will walk into blessings in the heart of your faith.

Faith allows your destination after walking through the valley to be a place where you will lend and not borrow. It is not just money that you will be able to lend to others. Time, encouragement, job positions, and so many other things will serve as blessings that you will have that you will be able to present to others. Your victory will serve as a testimony! Regardless of how difficult each step may seem as you walk through the valley, remember that it is serving as a test that God will turn into a testimony in your life. "The LORD makes firm the steps of the one who delights in him; though he may stumble, he will not fall, for the LORD upholds him with his hand" (Psalm 37:23-24 NIV).

Despite having to walk through the valley, keep in mind that there is another side to that valley. My friend, never forget that faith the size of a mustard seed is all you need to have God bless you to see the other side of your valley that is filled with green pastures. Some people see reaching a valley as a period that has come about to a sentence that God has written in their lives. Even so, your life is comprised of more than one sentence. Although God may put a period at one place in our lives, He follows that period with a capital letter, and He begins a new sentence in our lives.

In life, we often want what takes place to be like a book with a Table of Contents. We want to be able to look at what page a certain chapter of our lives will begin on and turn to that page with no problem. However, life is not a story that God tells in that fashion. He brings forth highs and lows, twists, and turns, and He makes it clear that walking with faith within our footsteps is spiritually beneficial. The story of our lives that God writes does not have a Table of Contents that we may view at our leisure, which is why we must trust Him.

When you take footsteps of faith as you walk through the valley that you are facing, you grow to appreciate trivial things that you once took for granted. Being able to physically walk was something that I once took for granted. However, after I sprained my ankle, I was not able to freely walk like I could before. After I was once again able to walk well, I began to park further away from my locations, take longer walking paths to my destinations, and jog more frequently. These were extra things that I did with my physical movement because I learned not to take it for granted.

Being able to physically do extra things when I regained my ability to walk was a success in my life. Although others may have only seen me as a man jogging along a trail or walking through the doors of a store from a far parking space, I knew my story. Every step I took had a story behind it. Also, every step you take as you are walking through your valley has a story behind it. My friend, every success has a story behind how it came forth. The next time you need something positive to motivate you as you walk through the valley in your life, let these words ring out within your mind: *I will make it through this valley! This is only temporary! The Lord will bless me to rise to new heights!*

Your time in the valley is only a temporary point in your life. It is not a permanent place where you must settle. Never forget that you are walking through the valley, not taking your final steps in the valley. I have found that the best way to adjust the way you walk is to learn how you are walking so that it may be changed if you want a change to come about in your life. If nothing else, you need to answer one question for yourself: *Am I walking by faith or by sight?* To put it another way, are you trusting God, no matter how your situation appears, or are you simply allowing what appears through the eyes of man to lead the steps you take? It is so easy to get caught up in believing what is right in front of you when you lack faith. Even so, if believing what is right in front of you was the best thing to do, how could there be multi-millionaires in the business world who were once turned down repeatedly before becoming successful?

Visualize an entrepreneur who had an idea for a product, but this person was repeatedly turned down by hundreds of possible supporters. Imagine a high number of individuals speaking negatively about the entrepreneur for stepping out on faith and leaving a "secure" job to become his or her own boss. Through the eyes of man, failure would be the only outcome for this person. However, as a result of keeping the faith, the entrepreneur gained the support of only 10 people before reaching the needed status to have the product bring about millions of dollars. Successful people in many areas are often able to identify with situations like these. The steps that you take should not be guided by what is naturally seen, but by faith that keeps the belief for greatness alive within you. "For we walk by faith, not by sight" (2 Corinthians 5:7 NKJV).

The valley itself is not the issue. Your journey through the valley is the issue. My friend, the steps you take through the valley are the issue. When you take footsteps of faith, you allow yourself to step beyond the natural realm and into the supernatural realm. By settling for the natural, you allow yourself to identify with the ordinary. On the other hand, when you do not settle for the natural, you rise to the supernatural. Being in the supernatural realm, you identify with the power of the extraordinary. With this spiritual identification, you will see the power of God in action!

Spiritual identification is something that many people can connect with when all is well, but it tends to be difficult when times are hard. I had the opportunity to meet a gentleman at a highly distinguished company, and the respect that his colleagues had for him was amazing. I could clearly see that his spiritual identification was a key point as to why he was so successful. When I learned about the foundation of his success, I was taken aback. He happened to be a wrongly convicted felon who was unable to find employment for a long period of time. However, after applying repeatedly to many companies for several months, he was contacted by two companies for an interview with each of them. It just so happened that he had interviews with the two companies on the same day within a matter of hours. One company turned him down after learning that he was a felon, but the other company gave him a chance by hiring him. After gaining the needed funds from his income to hire a well-established attorney, it was found that he was wrongly convicted. Following this, his record was cleared.

Soon after learning that he was wrongly convicted, the company that turned him down now wanted to hire him. Even so, he passed on the opportunity. A short time later, he helped his company gain controlling interest in the company that turned him down. While speaking with his employer after this took place, he expressed his gratefulness for having a second chance. He made it clear that if he did not have a second chance, he would not have gained the funds to hire an attorney of such high quality. If that did not happen, he likely would still have a bad record, and he would be someone who was continually overlooked when it came to employment. The employer told him that he believed in his innocence, and he wanted to give him the chance to prove his innocence. Within moments, the employer let the gentleman know that there was one thing that he could see that he had, which was what prompted him to hire the gentleman at the company: *faith*.

Faith is a spiritual tool that will legitimize the desires of your heart. Despite your time in the valley, God is orchestrating every step that you are taking with His divine hand. He makes your trials in pursuit of your goals become testimonies that epitomize His greatness. When you have faith, you will see a mess in one minute become a message in another minute.

Your walk through the valley may be God's way of placing you back on track after being lost in spiritual wilderness. There are times in life when we are lost, and we do not even realize it. God tends to use these as times when He steps into the situation so that He will guide our steps in the direction where they need to be. The steps you are taking as you walk through the valley will empower your faith and connection with our Heavenly Father. You may feel as if you are falling short of something that you truly desire. Even so, what you lack on one day can become an abundance on another day when you have faith.

Whatever you need, rest assured that our Heavenly Father will provide it. Whatever you want, rest assured that He will not hide it. In times of trouble, you do not have to cry because God is always your ally. As adversity rains upon you, just remember that you never cry alone because God is always on the throne. Keep in mind that God turns our disappointments into our appointments with blessings.

Man has often tried to imitate the power of God, but he has never even come close to scratching the surface of duplicating it. The greater glory of God always surpasses the limited power of man. Although man will try to hinder the happenings in your life, faith keeps you right in line with the blessings God has prepared for you. Faith brings about a stunning upset against the word "impossible" in the game of life because your trust rests upon the Lord. Whatever impossibility appears to sit in front of you, faith in the Lord to see you through it will make you victorious, regardless of how your situation may appear.

By not embracing a vision for your life, you may see what appears to be an emergency taking place that must be fixed immediately. Even so, an emergency to man is not an emergency to God. With trust in Him, the timing for your blessings is the right time. My friend, what seems impossible to the natural eye becomes reality to the path laid by God. Embrace your vision, keep the faith, and let God do His work.

When you have a vision for your life, you can move aside from the steering wheel and let God be the driver. Let the hand of God drive you where you need to be, as you allow faith to be the gas that moves you. My friend, let go of your problems and let God have His way. The battle is not for you to fight. It is for our Heavenly Father.

With God having His way in our lives, faith empowers the footsteps that we take as we walk through the valley. Never forget that faith is the common denominator between you and your challenges. It makes you ascend toward greater heights. As faith resides within your spirit, you will add together with the blessings that uplift you to reach much better places and subtract from the obstacles that try to hold you back.

Do not look back. Do not look down. Do not look over what you need to see. If you want to rise to a point of triumph, just look up to the Lord. Our Heavenly Father is on His throne steering your path. The walk that you are taking in the valley may seem difficult, but never forget that God has a reason for every step that you take. When you are walking, you are less likely to miss something that you would see if you were running. If we begin to move too fast, God tends to slow us down so that we will see something that we need to see in order to reach victory. Overlooking important points in life is often why we stumble. Even so, God will make a stumbling block in our lives today become a stepping stone toward greatness tomorrow. On a walk through the valley instead of a run, God leads us to see the things we need to see in order to reach victory.

The patterns of our footsteps go along with the spiritual maturity that comes to us over time. In our younger days, we may have a lack of understanding as to why God brings about the things that take place in our lives. Trials and tribulations taking place in our lives may appear as if God was simply turning away from our prayers. Nevertheless, as we mature over time, we can see that God is strengthening the faith within each footstep that we take as we walk through the valley. With this, we can turn away from the immaturity that holds us back in life. "When I was a child, I spoke as a child, I understood as a child, I thought as a child; but when I became a man, I put away childish things" (1 Corinthians 13:11 NKJV).

God prepares you for your walk through the valley, and He empowers you even more with each step you take. As we walk through our challenging times, we can see that walking through the valley is just as important as standing on the mountaintop of triumph. With faith residing in your spirit, you will begin to walk on the hills of hope, not wallow in the valley of defeat. Your walk through the valley is not just about where you are going, but also how you will get there. My friend, the faith within your spirit, the belief in your heart, and your prayers to the Lord will guide your steps through the valley and lead you to your mountaintop of triumph.

One problem that lives within the subconscious minds of so many people is that they cannot embrace progress and procrastination at the same time. Progress and procrastination cannot live side by side. Procrastination flows from doubt, while progress flows from faith.

My friend, do not let doubt deter you from your destiny. Belief in the greatness within you should be what drives you, not the belief of what others say about you. A person can tell you anything. What matters is whether you believe it. Trust God to move on your behalf and keep the faith that you will be blessed.

Although God has you walking through the valley, He is using every step you take as a journey to lead you toward your victory. Until you walk through the valley, you do not appreciate the mountaintop of triumph. The steps you take as you walk through the valley teach you to change the words "I can't" to "I will." Let this spiritual knowledge guide you to reach greater heights in life.

As you take footsteps while walking through the valley, always remain conscious of the type of spiritual shoes you are wearing. Are you wearing shoes of faith? Are you wearing shoes of hope? Are you wearing shoes of doubt? Are you wearing shoes of negativity? Always remember that one of the strongest influences of the spiritual shoes that you wear as you walk through the valley happens to be the people who surround you. Nevertheless, you may not even take the time to realize it.

The people who surround you are often those who influence the type of spiritual shoes that you wear as you walk through the valley due to their influence upon your mind. Times exist when people around you open the door to negativity. These types of people feed off steering you away from where you should be walking, and influence doubt and worry to serve as primary factors that bring about negativity in your life. Every so often, take the time to evaluate the people surrounding you. Are they building you up, or are they tearing you down? Do these people make you want to rise higher amid adversity, or lie down with feelings of defeat?

Spiritual ignorance tends to be a contributing factor to lessening faith. Do not allow this to happen to you. Be aware of who is around you, why they are around you, and whether they should be around you. If you find that the people surrounding you are bringing you down more than lifting you up, declare to yourself that it is time to make a change to the people in your circle.

In addition to the people who surround you, take the time to evaluate the situations surrounding you. Are you in a situation that you feel is too much for you? Why do you feel that it is too much for you? Have you turned your situation over to our Heavenly Father, or are you still trying to handle it on your own? No matter how big or small the situation happens to be, always approach it with God.

When a person or situation brings about negative feelings within your spirit or anger within your thoughts, take the time to mentally step back. Instead of always embracing what is around you, consider the source. Pay attention to who and what lifts you, as well as who and what brings you down. Search for good things that will make you rise higher in life, and how you can use these things to overcome the bad things that are trying to bring you down.

Focus on the good things that are present in your life, and how faith in God will turn the tide in your favor. My friend, despite what is negative in your life, there is still something positive to stand tall against the negative. By focusing on a negative situation or a demeaning person, you are bringing yourself down. Do not bring yourself down. Lift yourself up.

Never forget that even on what feels like the worst days of your life, God still sits high and looks low on His throne! Keeping this in mind, a key piece of advice that I have for you is to make sure that you begin each day of your life by making a connection with God. A few minutes of morning prayer have the power to block obstacles that may be awaiting you during the day. The way that you spend your morning often tells the story of how the rest of your day will take place. Knowing this, you must keep in mind the importance of every morning that God wakes you up.

Every morning that God wakes you up, He is doing so for a reason. By giving you another day of life, God is giving you another chance. No matter how big the obstacles in your life may seem, you have another chance for a reason. If the Lord meant for your obstacles to overpower you, He would not allow you to live another day with the opportunity to overpower your obstacles. Instead of sitting down in fear, stand up in praise. By using praise as your weapon, you will move forward to the mountaintop of victory.

Take your moments of worrying about your problems and turn them into a time of worshipping our Heavenly Father. Worship God! Praise God! Expect great things from God! When we rise in praise to our Heavenly Father, we see the good even in what could be seen as life's worst situations. By using praise as our weapon, we can see God's power in what is happening now, despite how our present situations may look on the surface. "I will call upon the LORD, who is worthy to be praised: so shall I be saved from mine enemies" (Psalm 18:3 KJV).

Storms will rage in your life that will thrust you into a walk through the valley. Do not let that stop you. Embrace your role as a victor, not a victim. The valley is not your stopping point in your life. It is not your destiny. God will provide you with spiritual funding that will empower you to walk through the valley, not to reside in the valley.

There have been days in my life when I have wondered how I would make it to the next hour, much less the next day. Times like these made me step back to see what God was showing me. My friend, you may have stepped into the valley one way, but following the direction in which God is leading you will make you step out in a better way. Despite how difficult your situation may seem on the surface to you, God will order your steps according to His will as you walk through the valley. He brought you into the valley, and He will bring you through the valley. Your steps in the valley are not working against you. They are working for you. "And we know that in all things God works for the good of those who love Him, who have been called according to His purpose" (Romans 8:28 NIV).

Each step that you take on your path in life is a part of God's plan for you. No point in your life happens without a reason. There is a reason why God positioned every place that you will encounter as a part of your life, including your time in the valley. If you were not supposed to be in the valley, then you would not be there. Every crook and turn that you are taking in the valley is for a reason. Let God do His work with His plan for your life, as you keep the faith in Him.

Do not let your walk through the valley upset you. Rest assured that God is using the valley as a part of His plan for you. Think of lifting weights in a gym. If you were to stay away from lifting weights, then your muscles would not grow. On the same accord, if you did not have hard times to endure, then you would not have greater heights to reach.

The steps that you are taking in your life at this very moment may be leading you toward blessings ahead. Keep the faith that your steps through the valley are serving as points of growth for you. Your movement through the valley is positioning you for excellence ahead of you in the future. Your time in the valley is preparing you for the greatness that God has ready to shine through you. All God is asking from you is to keep the faith. Trust Him to order your steps.

If there were no valleys to walk through, there would be no mountaintops to reach. If life had no challenges, there would be no victories to achieve. Your valley is the obstacle in your life that God is using to bring you to greater heights. Although you may feel limited by a struggle at this exact second, do not let that stop you. Limitations are not the end of your path in life. Stand strong and stand tall against any limitation that approaches you.

As you take footsteps of faith, keep in mind that it is not just the shoes you wear, but also how you walk in those shoes that matters. Imagine having just bought the best shoes you could find, and then putting those new shoes on to wear. Then, you walk in place. What is the matter with that picture? Although you are moving, you are not moving anywhere new. Now, picture yourself in this same situation, but you are walking backward instead of forward. What is the problem there? Although you are also moving in this situation, you are moving in the wrong direction. Both scenarios have the problem of walking the wrong way instead of the right way. This is why it is very important to look to the Lord for guidance as we take the footsteps of faith.

While you are in the valley, there may be days when you are hurting so much that it feels like taking another step on your walk would be too much to bear. It may seem as if the most logical thing to do is to fall in defeat, and not take another step on your walk through the valley. Nevertheless, remember that you are not walking logically. You are walking spiritually. My friend, embrace peace in your life. Embrace hope in your life. Embrace faith in your life. Embrace the power of God in your life. Allow the Lord to guide your steps and let Him lead you.

Despite how badly things may appear for you as you walk through the valley, keep in mind that the fruits of the valley will flourish inside of you. God has great things for you to take with you as products of your walk through the valley. As much as we need fruit within us, fruit does not grow within our spirits as we stand on the mountaintop. Fruit grows in the valley, and He blesses us with that fruit as we take our steps.

Although the valley may seem to be a place of great heartache, it is still a place of growth. No point of your pain is being wasted. Growth is taking place on your behalf as you are empowered with spiritual fruits. Resilience is a spiritual fruit that grows within you as you walk through the valley. Maturity is a spiritual fruit that grows within you as you walk through the valley. Strength is a spiritual fruit that grows within you as you walk through the valley. Regardless of how your situation may seem on the surface, trust that the Lord has fruit for your soul to receive that will guide you toward your blessings.

Fruit is not always able to be seen when we look at a certain place on a farm. A specific place on a farm may be where the fruit will eventually be seen, yet it is not able to be immediately seen. There is a certain timeframe in which the fruit must first grow. It must reach a point of maturity before it can manifest into a new place of living. Before coming into a new place of living, the fruit must gain a new level of strength. Just as this happens to fruit that ripens on a farm, this also happens to you as you walk through the valley. Like the fruit will sprout from underground and reach a new place of life, the same will happen to you after the Lord blesses you with maturity, growth, and strength. "You did not choose me, but I chose you and appointed you so that you might go and bear fruit—fruit that will last—and so that whatever you ask in my name the Father will give you" (John 15:16 NIV).

Pause with me for a moment. Think of your favorite fruit. How was your favorite fruit able to reach its full maturation so that you could eat it? The fruit simply came from a seed that grew in the soil before becoming what you know it to be. That very fruit grows through its own valley for it to become what you need it to be when you eat it. Just as you can physically grow by eating physical fruit in daily life, God blesses you with spiritual fruit so that you are able to grow spiritually as you walk through the valley.

We often do not think of the complex process that it takes for our favorite fruit to grow before we eat it. At the same time, we often do not think of the fruit that God is feeding us as we walk through the valley where He has placed us. My friend, if God blesses you with the outcome of a complex process physically, He will certainly bless you with the outcome of a complex process spiritually. Even so, to gain the outcome of a complex spiritual process, we must understand that we must go through a period of maturation, growth, and strengthening. Being in the valley serves this purpose. No moment in the valley is in vain.

As you walk through the valley, remember that you will reach higher places in life when you trust in the Lord. Never forget that our Heavenly Father has positioned you in a place where there is nowhere for you to look for guidance but up to Him. When you look up to Him, you will see that He is giving you direction. By looking up to God, He then leads you forward in life, not backward. With the steps you take, as you walk through the valley, God feeds you the fruits of maturity, growth, and strength that you need for you to be led out of the valley. By feeding you with these fruits as you walk through the valley, God also feeds you with knowledge of how to use these fruits in future times of need.

By keeping faith within your spirit as you walk through the valley, you are leading yourself to the mountaintop. The view from the mountaintop is peaceful, serene, and pleasing. Although your walk through the valley will have been a challenging point in your life, the lessons gained from the steps you took will empower you with knowledge of how to return to the mountaintop if you ever fall.

It is essential to know how to return to the mountaintop if there is ever a need. Imagine that someone gave you a large sum of money, but you had no idea how this person was able to make that large sum of money. In this situation, you would be able to live years upon years of a lifestyle associated with a large sum of money. Now, imagine that you lost that large sum of money within a matter of seconds. What would you do? If you knew how the money was made in the first place, you would simply need to follow the same path taken to get it the first time. However, with no idea of how to make money, you would be facing a tremendous problem that you would not know how to overcome.

The mountaintop is the place where we all want to be. Each time we close our eyes, and we are in the valley, and then we open our eyes again and we are still in the valley seems like one hard time after another. Despite this, just remember that every second of life is a second of God's work in action. He has you in the valley so that you will rise to the mountaintop.

What is the mountaintop that you want to stand on? Is it overcoming a health issue? Could it be becoming employed again after being laid off? Perhaps becoming successful as an entrepreneur? Take the time to envision it. Close your eyes with me for the next 60 seconds and picture yourself standing on *your* mountaintop. Now, open your eyes. How did it feel to no longer be in the valley? What was it like to stand on *your* mountaintop? My friend, the same feeling of grace that you had during that 60 seconds on *your* mountaintop should be the same feeling that you have when you need to stir up the faith within you.

Think of the last time you needed to stir up your faith. What did you do? How did it turn out? My friend, whether it turned out well or not so well, there are two things that I want you to do on a regular basis: *meditate and study*. Meditate on the Word of God. Study the Word of God. By doing this, you will stir up faith within your spirit in all sets of situations. These spiritual exercises will allow you to see that the power of God is greater than every set of circumstances that may come before you.

Spiritual authenticity lives within you. Genuineness exists within your soul. The Lord made you true to the nature, personality, and values that He wants you to have. The happenings in your life have a direct response from your soul. What the Lord places within you serves as powerful tools for you to combat whatever stands between you and your blessings.

Instead of spending time lying in bed at night restlessly worrying about your problems or walking throughout the day anxiously agonizing over your difficulties, I have a new spiritual strategy to strengthen your soul. I want you to put a new spiritual exercise into practice for the next 10 days to feed your soul. Read 2 Bible scriptures when you wake up in the morning. After this, take 60 seconds to close your eyes and meditate upon those scriptures. Then, think of 3 words that best describe your spiritual understanding of those scriptures. If any point occurs throughout the day when a challenge comes before you, reflect upon those 3 words to strengthen your mind so that you will positively feed your soul. At a point of your choosing during the day, read 2 more Bible scriptures. Follow the same process that you used during your morning spiritual exercise. Lastly, read 2 more Bible scriptures at night before you go to bed. Carry out this exercise once again. If a time occurs at night when you wake up thinking of difficulties in your life, enact the exercise of reflecting upon your chosen words so that you will once again combat those negative thoughts. "In thee, O LORD, do I put my trust; let me never be ashamed: deliver me in thy righteousness" (Psalm 31:1 KJV).

Let these new practices in your life become what you use to allow you to stand your ground with faith. Allow these spiritual exercises to encourage a sense of spiritual urgency that prompts your faith to knock down any doubt or worry that may exist within you. No matter how challenging or difficult a situation may appear, studying the Word of God and meditation upon the Word of God will bring awesome changes into your life. You will become spiritually conditioned to see that one moment of your life may be hard, but the power of God will bring you through it. "Blessed is the man that trusteth in the LORD, and whose hope the LORD is" (Jeremiah 17:7 KJV).

Pause with me for a moment. Look in the mirror. Who do you see? Nobody but you. You are the **only** person who you see. At the same time, you are **not** alone. God is with you. Although you do not physically see our Heavenly Father, He is always with you in spirit. In the best of times and the worst of times, God is with you. Whether the sun shines brightly throughout the day or if rain pours down with each second, God is with you. Knowing this, let your trust in God empower you to have faith that will maintain itself within your spirit and grow stronger each day.

Faith makes your soul gravitate toward peace. Fear makes you have a doubtful mind filled with worry. To walk through the valley instead of remaining at a stagnant point in the valley, you cannot wear the perfect shoe size of faith and fear at the same time. As faith resides within your spirit, peace will overpower uncertainty so that you will take risks that will make you rise to greater heights. When you take risks, you remove limits. You cannot be limitless when you hold onto things that limit you.

The steps you take as you walk through the valley tend to be what God uses to free you from things in your life that limit you. The limits in your life are chains that hold you in specific spots so that you will not walk through the valley, but instead remain unable to move forward. Regardless of what chains are present in your life, God uses your faith to unchain you. No matter how difficult the steps you take as you walk through the valley may seem, keep the faith that God is working out your situation in your favor. Smile as you take your steps, not just when you reach the finish line.

Too often we see a point in life that we missed as one of the greatest limits in our lives. That point often plays out repeatedly as the reason we did not make a certain turn. Nevertheless, a turn that you miss could end up being the right turn that God intends for you to make. Do not let what you see at this moment overpower what you believe. What God has ordained for you will take place, despite how things may seem now. Your timetable is not always the same as God's timetable, but God's timetable is the best timetable for you. Instead of allowing your mind to serve as an obstacle for you, make it a driving force that makes you progress. Do not let the way you think limit you. Let the way you think empower you.

One of the worst ways we limit ourselves is with our worries regarding time. As we worry too much, we lead to one of life's biggest limitations: *stress*. A gentleman who I am aware of allowed stress in his life to lead to him to have a bleeding ulcer. Thousands upon thousands of dollars were spent on medical treatments. Even so, he embraced studying the Word of God and meditation upon the Word of God. These practices brought great changes into his life. Faith became a pivotal aspect within his soul. Having faith took away the significant amount of stress in his life that was weighing him down. Faith led to his medical treatments going well, and he no longer had issues with a bleeding ulcer. To this day, he gives his testimony over and over about how faith empowered him to overcome his health problems. My friend, faith keeps you in the fight, despite how things may seem.

Time and time again we embrace the ease of looking down upon how things appear to us on the surface. We focus on what we lack in our lives. Even so, we must learn to step back from this. It is not always about what you have, but how you use what you have that matters. Think of how things could be different for two people who have the exact same amount of money. One person may use their money toward paying bills and buying luxuries, while another person may use that exact same amount of money to pay bills and make investments. What is likely to happen? The person who used the money that was not spent on bills to make investments is much more likely to have financial prosperity than the one who put money toward buying luxuries. Why is there a difference? It is because of *how* the two people used what they had. These two people used the money differently because of *how* they saw it. One person may have thought that investing was "too much," while the other may have thought that investing was ***not*** "too much." To be successful at whatever we pursue, we cannot let our focus on what we do not have overshadow our focus on what we do have.

Focusing on how you will use what you have is a powerful strategy. This makes us use what we have in order to move toward greater things in life. The thing I love best about this type of focus is that it motivates us not to settle for having a "decent" state of living. Being satisfied with what is "decent" can hold you back from achieving your best. Why does an athlete put in extra time outside of practice? It is because the athlete does not want to be a "decent" athlete. This person wants to advance athletically. The athlete wants to be the *best* that he or she can be. Why does someone who has a vast amount of knowledge not stop with a job that pays an amount of money that stands out very well to others, but rather opens his or her own company using that very knowledge? It is because this entrepreneur did not want to have a "decent" job being just another worker at someone else's company.

Think of one thing in your life that you were "decent" at doing, but you feel you could have put in much more effort to be GREAT at doing. For the next 60 seconds, close your eyes and reflect upon what you did not do to make yourself GREAT at this, and what you feel hindered you at just being "decent." Open your eyes now. Think of 3 words that come to mind when you reflect upon what would have made you GREAT. Now, think of 3 words that come to mind when you reflect upon what hindered you to not go past being "decent."

For the next 7 days, I want you to set aside a time of optimism. I want you to set aside 60 seconds of each day to have a time for daily reflection pertaining to this matter. Let your time of reflection allow you to think about why you felt one set of words impacted your life to stop you at being "decent," and why the other set of words could empower you toward greatness. During this time, I want you to close your eyes and meditate on what actions you can take to make the 3 words of hindrance become overpowered by the 3 words of greatness. After this 7-day time span, I want you to have a plan of how you can literally and figuratively step forward with your faith. Pursuing your education? Changing jobs? Opening your own business? Revisiting a goal that you turned away from when it seemed to be too much to handle? Figure out what you want to step toward, create a plan for how you will get there, and move confidently with your faith!

For you to embrace yourself as an individual who will reach greater heights, you must first transform your mindset from where it is to where it needs to be. An employee cannot be a business owner by thinking like an employee. A patient lying in a hospital bed cannot be an individual who walks amongst those in good health by thinking like someone who will never be released from a hospital. A wrongly convicted prisoner cannot become a free individual by thinking like someone who will never be released from prison. My friend, you are transformed when your mind is renewed by trusting in God. When your trust resides in God, your mind is not limited by challenges. Move past the limits you have today. Rise into a limitless tomorrow.

What habits empower you? What habits disempower you? To transform your mind, strengthen the habits that empower you. Weaken the habits that disempower you. To help with this, I want you to engage in an activity for the next 10 days. Write 1 thing that disempowers you and stick it on your mirror. Next, write 1 thing that empowers you and place it over the thing that disempowers you. Allow this activity to reroute your mind and empower your soul. By doing this, you will transform your mind in an optimistic, positive fashion. "And be not conformed to this world: but be ye transformed by the renewing of your mind, that ye may prove what is that good, and acceptable, and perfect, will of God" (Romans 12:2 KJV).

Too often in life we settle with what is "decent" because of mistakes we have made in the past. My friend, always remember that the mercy of God is greater than any mistakes that we could ever make. Regardless of what you may have done in the times before you, focus instead on what God will do for you in the times ahead of you. Follow the Lord, and let His guidance lead the new steps that you will take. Do not let what has happened hold you back from what may happen. Always keep the faith.

There tend to be times in life when we want to act first and think about our actions later. The problem with this is that two things in life go hand in hand: *choices and outcomes*. This becomes very clear when the steps you take are shifted beyond your control. As you walk through the valley, you will reach a fork in the road. Be sure to stop and sincerely consider the outcomes of your choices. Keep in mind that a turn you take at your fork in the road can make all the difference for you.

I have had points in my own life when I have had to pause because of a lack of clarity, and even stop because of that lack of clarity. These have been points when all I could do was come before the Lord and ask Him for guidance. As we drive in everyday life, we come to lights that give us direction. *Go. Yield. Stop.* In the same way, we come to lights that God has placed before us that give us direction on our spiritual roads of life. During the time that this takes place, we must realize that there is a benefit to following the lights that God gives us. There is a purpose behind why the light is green when it is green. There is a purpose behind why the light is yellow when it is yellow. There is a purpose behind why the light is red when it is red. My friend, God has a purpose for why He allows us to move forward. He has a reason for why He makes us slow down. The Lord has a motive for why He brings us to a stopping point when He does. God is strategic with His moves, and He is perfect with His timing.

It is often easy to say that you will go when the Lord tells you to go, but it is much different to go when the light leads you to spiritually move. At the same time, it is often easy to say that you will slow down when the Lord tells you to slow down, but it is much different when the light leads you to spiritually yield. On the same token, it is often easy to say that you will stop when the Lord tells you to stop, but it is much different when the light leads you to spiritually stop. The spiritual lights shine when God commands them, and we must learn to follow the direction that God gives.

To go through the light, you must make the decision to go through it. To yield to the light, you must make the decision to slow down when you approach the light. To stop at the light, you must make the decision to no longer move. Even so, you must have certainty behind what you do, not uncertainty. You cannot hesitate and expect greatness to burst throughout your life. Many times, we move with hesitation because we are afraid of rising above an ordinary life. However, *ordinary* cannot exist while *extraordinary* exists. Ordinary steps bring ordinary outcomes, but bold steps bring extraordinary outcomes. When you are a bold person who takes needed risks, you will experience God's unheard-of excellence in your life. When you want the best, you should strive for the best.

Each day on the road of your life, you are putting words behind your spiritual narrative. When your steps move in cohesion with God's guidance, you show your confidence in His leadership. By following the lights that God has in front of you, your valley becomes a temporary space, not a permanent place. Moving in unity with the spiritual lights that God places in front of you allows you to gain spiritual refreshment. You can live every moment of your life to the fullest, regardless of how good or bad it may seem. Always remember that your actions demonstrate your expectations. Let the actions you take at this moment prepare you for greatness in the moments ahead.

Your walk through the valley builds a new foundation upon your path. The stumbles on your walk through the valley will make you stand taller and make your steps become stronger. Never let a stumble at one point make you fall. Stand tall. Stand strong. Let your confidence in the Lord rest upon you even at times when life appears to be too much for you to bear. Regardless of the challenges that stand before you, hold strong to the belief that God has better things prepared for you on the other side of the challenges.

Challenges are often what precede our blessings. Nevertheless, when a challenge enters our lives, this makes it so easy to fall into failure due to doubts holding us down. Even so, we must see the challenge as a gift, because God has the gift of our blessings following that challenge. Hold strong to the belief that faith makes *you* present challenges to your obstacles. This keeps your obstacles from challenging you. Faith makes you internalize confidence, but fear makes you internalize doubt. Faith gives you opportunities. Faith gives you options. Fear gives you limitations. Fear draws the line in the sand to hold you back from your blessings. Faith and fear cannot peacefully coexist. My friend, do not let doubt overpower your dreams. Let your faith overpower your doubts.

When doubts are overpowered, blessings come to fruition. When worries are overpowered, blessings come to fruition. Do not tolerate being treated like a piece of mediocrity by your fears. Remember that you are a child of God. Always hold strong to God's plan for your life. Although you may experience a wrinkle in your walk at certain times, it is not meant to stop you. Nothing and no one can hold the blessings that God has in His plan away from you. Regardless of the obstacles that may come about in your life, God will shine light on your footsteps as you walk through the valley.

Do not concern yourself with what you cannot control. Whatever exists in your life that you cannot control, trust that God will control it for you. Instead of being anxious about your challenges, remember that faith turns anxiety into actions on your behalf. If everything was going well, you would not need to rise above your situation. No matter how bad your challenges may appear, keep the faith. Relax and trust that God will bring light into your life in the midnight hour.

"The people walking in darkness have seen a great light; on those living in the land of deep darkness a light has dawned" (Isaiah 9:2 NIV).

What serves as the valley that you are walking through today will soon become an entrance to the mountaintop where you will stand with victory in your days to come. When faith resides within you, God will lead you into a gateway of blessings. He has an entrance into your blessings waiting for you as a gift of your trust in Him. My friend, your steps in the valley will become your standing point on the mountaintop when you trust in God. Never forget that your time in the valley is temporary. Embrace the belief that trouble in your life today will become triumph in your days ahead. The steps you take as you walk through the valley will be transformed into a place where you will victoriously stand on the mountaintop when you have faith as small as a mustard seed. "I will return her vineyards to her and transform the Valley of Trouble into a gateway of hope" (Hosea 2:15 NLT).

Chapter Five

MY STRUGGLE TOWARD SUCCESS

Immobilization. **Devastation. Frustration.** What makes you stop the things you are doing? When are you devastated in life? Why are you emotionally distressed at certain times? The need to answer questions like these steers us toward why there is a significant need for faith in our lives. Challenging limitations may manifest daily, but it is up to us regarding how we will face them.

Financial challenges may be a limitation that enters your life. A pandemic may come about that leads to you being laid off due to the great financial downfall of your employer. With this, the pandemic may open the door to you having to be at home more than usual. Although you may be at home for long periods of time searching for a new job, a life-altering point may take place during this time, as well. You may also come across newly found free time aside from your job search to apply the knowledge that you have to start your own business online. This could set the path for you to open a shipping company that becomes a highly successful business that your former employer must now depend upon for success.

Imagine your former employer walking through a door to meet and thank you for taking on a new contract with his company. Moments later, he learns that the person he laid off is now making millions of dollars all because of his or her efforts after being laid off from the company. Envision your former employer being in awe of the knowledge that you have been placed back into the company's budget at an exponential financial rate. Instead of making the small paycheck you once made as an employee, you are now making millions as your own boss. "In all this, you greatly rejoice, though now for a little while you may have had to suffer grief in all kinds of trials. These have come so that the proven genuineness of your faith—of greater worth than gold, which perishes even though refined by fire—may result in praise, glory, and honor when Jesus Christ is revealed" (1 Peter 1:6-7 NIV).

Learn to praise God for what you have instead of complaining about what you do not have. Love the valley that you are walking through. Embrace the spiritual knowledge that the way out of the valley is through the valley. It is a journey to your destination, and your time on your journey will progress much smoother if you love it instead of loathing it. Although your time in the valley may be made of the most challenging days of your life, still give God praise. Praise God in times of peace and pain. God will bless you with divine connections that will allow you to rise to greater heights when the steps you take are made with faith.

When you have faith, you are able to turn what is pitiful at one step into what is powerful at another step. Taking one step forward with faith makes you one step closer to your higher destination of victory. By embracing faith within your spirit, you will see God bringing you closer to a point as opposed to man bringing you closer to a point. Always remember that just because something is closer does not mean that it is better. An outcome being close in the eyes of man is not necessarily the outcome that you should choose. Sometimes going the extra mile is worth it. Do not judge your situation only by what is seen through the natural eye.

What is further with the Lord is always better than what is closer with man. Taking what is closer with man tends to have an outcome that is much less than what it could be. Do not settle for what is less than your best. Do not compromise for what is less than what you can accomplish. When you compromise with a challenge, you leave the door open for that challenge to come back into your life. Never forget that God's forecast is not defined by man's forecast. Although man may see you at a lower place in life than where you are capable of being, God may plan for you to reach much greater heights. Instead of settling for limitations in life, rise above them.

Embrace a bounce-back mentality instead of falling into a finale. For every second that you are down, vow to yourself that you will rise again. Shake off your disappointments and stand up with strength. Although days will exist when you will walk through a valley in your life, hold onto the belief that there will be better days ahead. Declare to yourself that you will one day stand strong on the mountaintop of triumph.

Faith has a big adversary when it comes to allowing you to reach your greatest heights in life: *fear*. Many people are highly capable of doing great things in life, but fear makes them settle for much less. Although settling may be appealing to the natural eye, it is limiting to the growth of your spirit. One person may be much more qualified than another to be the leader of a particular department. Even so, fear may be the reason why the more qualified person is just another worker, and the less qualified person holds the title of the leader. Some people are fearful of success, which holds them down in life. Fear of how things may not go in one's favor is a key limitation in life.

Having fear instead of faith within your spirit makes you worry that shame is what you will bear in the end. The fear of what others will think of you can hold great power in your life if you allow it to have that power. There are so many times when what we think of ourselves is led by what others think of us. *I would try it, but I would be ashamed if it did not work out. It would be nice to do that, but it would be embarrassing if I could not do it.* Thoughts like these are what serve as limitations that stop highly qualified people from rising to their best. These thoughts make people fearful of success. When all is said and done, the way you think can be your best friend or your worst enemy. My friend, let faith be what resides within your spirit, not fear. Regardless of how things turn out, do not hold your head down in shame. Lift your head up with trust in the Lord.

Do not let your circumstances make you a victim. Embrace trust in the Lord to make you victorious over whatever comes before you. God will afford you opportunities that you have never imagined could happen. Trust God's timing. The pain that comes through your footsteps as you walk through the valley has a spiritual purpose of preparing you for better times ahead. If no pain existed in the valley, there would be no gain leading you to higher ground. Let your faith overpower your pain. Your pain has possibilities when you have faith. Take the needed steps to turn your pain into prosperity. Turn your pain into praise. Delight in your love of God. "The LORD makes firm the steps of the one who delights in him; though he may stumble, he will not fall, for the LORD upholds him with his hand" (Psalm 37:23-24 NIV).

You cannot have a limited perception of the power that God has placed within you. My friend, you must look at life through the eyes of faith to rise toward greater heights. Faith removes the spiritual astigmatism that may be clouding what you see before you. Regardless of the blurred vision that the natural eye may give you, the eyes of faith will spiritually treat the imperfections that cause the blur that you may have as you view the blessings ahead of you. "I will lift up mine eyes unto the hills, from whence cometh my help.

My help cometh from the LORD, which made heaven and earth" (Psalm 121:1-2 KJV).

Never forget that your walk through the valley is only a temporary period of your life. When faith resides within your spirit, God will empower you to move beyond the valley. Walking through the valley is often a period in life when a person wants to give up, regardless of how close a blessing happens to be. Walking through the valley tends to be seen by many as a point of interruption in life that cannot be overcome. Even so, an interruption may turn out to be an inspiration. Time after time when we see interruptions in our lives, we view them as stopping points. When an interruption in life appears to be too much, we want to simply lie down to the challenge it brings. However, a challenge from one view is an opportunity from another view.

Free your mind to see what God is showing you during the interruption that He has placed in your life. If your mind is blind, you will not see what is in front of you. If your mind is blind to the path before you, your eyes will be blind to your steps. Free your mind to our Heavenly Father! As difficult as the steps that you take as you walk through the valley may seem, rest assured that God has a purpose behind them. Never forget that God is purposeful with everything that He does. No step that He has you to take as you walk through the valley is without a purpose. Nothing in your life takes place for no reason.

Things in your life may feel empty and seem as if they are only holding you back. My friend, emptiness is not a part of your life. What appears empty in your life is where it is because it is waiting for God to put something there to fill the space with greatness. What should you do about it? Be purposeful with your faith. Be intentional with your faith. Regardless of what it may seem that you lack, keep the faith! Regardless of who seems to be against you, keep the faith! No matter how dim things may seem on the surface, keep the faith! Rest assured that God will take you from mediocrity to more than enough. "Thou preparest a table before me in the presence of mine enemies: thou anointest my head with oil; my cup runneth over" (Psalm 23:5 KJV).

There are many times in life when we only see the final product of something that has taken place. Pause with me for a moment. Picture what a tall bridge looks like. Now, picture tall buildings in the downtown skyline of a city. Next, picture a community full of homes surrounding the area. Have those things always been where they are? *No.* Whether those areas were previously filled with trees or if they were clear spaces of land, they were empty when it comes to what is there now. Just like there are things in your life that may seem empty now, there was a time when the spaces that you just mentally pictured were empty. However, someone had in mind what those empty spaces would be like when they were one day filled with great things. Whenever you seem to feel as if emptiness is overflowing in your life, allow your mind to see what great things may one day fill it with existence. See blessings overflowing upon you.

One of the best ways to overpower feelings of emptiness is to have a time of reflection. For the next 7 days, I want you to add another task to your period of optimism. Write down 5 positive points about yourself each day. Allow these to be points that you feel are great things about yourself, and keep in mind why these are great things about who you are. During this period each day, take 60 seconds to verbally affirm these 5 positive points to yourself. Speak these 5 positive points to yourself with confidence. Let the meaning behind each of these points instill itself into your spirit. Permit these 5 positive points to improve who you are instead of allowing negative things to gain space in your mind. Reflect intensely during this time. For each second of your reflection, let this be a time of spiritual self-evaluation. Allow this to become a medicine for your spiritual well-being. When your spiritual well-being improves, your life will improve. You will begin to see the space of emptiness in your life become a place of optimism.

On many days of our lives, we are so busy that setting aside a time of reflection is the last thing on our list of what we will do. Even so, a time of reflection is a very important time for us to have in our lives. As we reflect, it gives us time to counteract what could otherwise lead to low self-esteem, depression, pessimism, and so many other negative aspects of life. When we take the time to reflect, we have the chance to see things again that we once saw. My friend, when God gives you the chance to see something again, look at it from a different view. Look from a different angle. If you do not, you will still see the same thing you saw before. Keep in mind that when God shows you something again, it is not simply for you to see it the exact same way.

Pause with me for a moment. Close your eyes and think about something that happened in your life that once appeared to be a negative point for you, but it later turned out to be something in your favor. What would have occurred if this point that you thought was negative happened to take place how you wanted it to take place instead of how it did in God's plan for you? At this very moment, would what you are thinking about still have turned out to be a blessing for you? This is just one example of how when we take the time to reflect upon things that have happened in our lives, we are able to see how things turn around in our favor when we have faith. Looking at situations in our lives from a different view shows us that although something may appear to be against us from one angle, viewing the same thing from another angle shows us that it is for us in the long run.

Setting aside time to reflect during your day is one of the most powerful tools to counteract issues with mental health. It empowers your hope. It empowers your faith. It empowers your expectancy. It empowers your optimism. Walking through the valley tends to be a time of life that is very difficult for a person's mental health. However, reflection and faith are things that come hand and hand to let your mental health rest upon a solid spiritual foundation. The valley is a low place in life that leaves you with only two options: *look down and stay where you are or look up and rise above where you are.* When faith sheds light onto your path, there is nowhere to go but up. During your time of reflection, always keep this in mind.

Days may come about in your life when it appears that you have no words for your situation, only tears. My friend, God understands our tears. Tears speak loudly and clearly to God. Although you may not verbally say anything, your tears are clearly speaking to God. This feeds into my belief of the need to set aside a time for reflection so that you will clear your mind and strengthen your faith. By having this connection with God, you will know that the tears that escape from within you are words that are spiritually communicated to God.

Life as a follower of God has its challenges. However, God is right there for you when any challenges present themselves. Too often we simply want to think of ourselves as followers of God when it comes to having nothing in our lives but blessings. However, we tend to forget that to reach the blessings that await us on the mountaintop, there are steps for us to take in the valley. Strong steps do not come from merely standing on the mountaintop. Strong steps come from walking through the valley. The steps you take as you walk through the valley make you appreciate where you will stand when you reach the mountaintop.

Regardless of how difficult your set of circumstances may seem, rest assured that the pain that comes with the steps you are taking is placing you closer to the blessings that God has waiting for you. Your challenges are being used to place you closer to your blessings. Your problems are being used to place you closer to your blessings. Days may exist when you are able to see that God is growing you as you walk through the valley just as He grows fruit. Even so, days may also exist when vagueness behind God's reasoning for why you are walking through the valley overwhelms you. Either way, keep the faith. Look to God for understanding. Pray to God for understanding.

God is open to our prayers, and knowledge is certainly something that we need to have. When you understand what God is doing in your life, walking through the valley becomes much easier to do. Although you will not understand all of God's ways, He will provide you with spiritual understanding to the extent that you are able to follow His orders. Instead of giving up, you will take the steps you need to take to reach your blessings. Gaining knowledge from the Lord is one of the most beneficial things that you can do. I cannot say enough that there are very capable people in this world, but they lack the knowledge needed to get to higher stages in life. Do not let that be you. Pray to God. Trust in God. Believe in God.

One of the most powerful points of understanding that God gives us is that we must apply the knowledge that He gives us. My friend, knowledge is power. With this, applying knowledge is one of the most powerful things that you can do. Just as prayer to the Lord grants you understanding and knowledge, studying the Word of God coincides with this so that you will apply your knowledge. Make it a regular practice in your life to study the Word of God and pray to God so that you will have knowledge, and you will effectively apply that knowledge to advance yourself in life. My friend, keep in mind that spiritual knowledge is not powerful when it is not applied.

Being a spiritually knowledgeable person is one of the most powerful blessings to have. Nevertheless, we must apply the knowledge that God gives us. My friend, you could have all the knowledge in the world throughout every second of the day, but it is worthless if you do not use it. Keep in mind that it is not what you know, but what you do with it that counts. The knowledge that you have must be applied effectively. If you have knowledge and you do not apply it in a way that advances you in life, you might as well not have it at all. As you apply your knowledge, you powerfully connect your faith with your works. Faith is the light that drives you, and your works serve as the action that God requires of you. From this, God will lead you into your blessings. "But be doers of the word, and not hearers only, deceiving yourselves" (James 1:22 NKJV).

Despite how your days may appear, look to God for spiritual intuition regarding the happenings in your life. Follow God's instructions with each step you take. God is writing your spiritual narrative, so it is always best to look to Him for direction. My friend, He will lead and guide you toward greatness. You may dislike the traffic on the road of your life but remember that God is the driver.

Remove the worry from your mind because the driver has everything under control. God is not only the driver, but He also controls the traffic. With such a powerful combination guiding you, there is no need for you to worry.

When things take place in life, your words often express how you feel about the situation. Not only do you express how you feel through what you have to say, but there is a very important person who hears what you have to say: *you*. The first person who hears what you have to say is you. My friend, do not just think of your words as a form of communication with others. Your words are also a form of communication with yourself.

Each word you speak flows through you and back into you. Never verbalize negativity or pessimism. Verbalize positiveness and optimism. Do not talk yourself out of victory. When you allow your words to verbalize defeat before you even make one step toward victory, there is no use even making one step toward the possibility of becoming a victor. With beliefs that are preparing defeat to be the outcome of your situation, faith is not the driving force within you. By preparing for defeat, you are allowing fear to overpower your faith. Fear overwhelms you to accept pessimistic beliefs, while faith motivates you to reach beyond limitations. Fear floods your mind with worry, but faith soothes your mind with peace.

Let your faithful prayers to the Lord be on the same wavelength as the words that come from your mouth regarding what is taking place in your life. When your walk through the valley appears to be too much to bear, speak these words: *I did not come this far just to stop here! God has great things planned for me!* No matter what potholes you experience on the drive through your journey, always remember that the Lord has brought about miraculous moments in the lives of His followers. "For I will pour water on the thirsty land, and streams on the dry ground; I will pour out my Spirit on your offspring, and my blessing on your descendants" (Isaiah 44:3 NIV).

Never put the breath of life behind negative words about yourself. Do not let negative words about who you are flow through your mouth. When you allow negative words to come from your lips, you give life to negativity being at the forefront of your life. Open your lips and let statements of triumph flow through you. Allow words of victory to come through you. When you verbalize victory as a key point in your future, you take spiritual steps toward victory.

The words you speak invite victory or defeat into your life. How often do you see a team walk onto the field expressing words of defeat before even playing the game? Do you regularly see highly accomplished people in the business world sharing how speaking words of pessimism are what made them successful? These are not things that you see take place from successful individuals. People who have achieved success are not the same people who speak negativity over themselves. Just as well-accomplished people speak words of optimism, you must also speak words of the same nature. Speak victory into existence! Speak excellence into existence! Give life to your blessings! Let the words that come from your tongue boost you to greater heights in life!

Give life to the greatness that lives within you by speaking it through your words. The more you give life to your own greatness through what you have to say about yourself, the more you will believe it. Let your speech of your very own words make you believe the best about yourself. Allow the words that flow from your tongue to steer you toward greater heights in your life, not beneath the level of excellence that God created for you. Speak victory over who you are! Speak abundance over who you are! Speak greatness over who you are! "From the fruit of their mouth a person's stomach is filled; with the harvest of their lips they are satisfied" (Proverbs 18:20 NIV).

You cannot prophesy struggles and reach success. You cannot speak mediocrity into existence and expect greatness to be your outcome. You cannot speak a fall in your future and expect a rise ahead of you. Do not invite defeat into your life through your words. Invite victory into your life through your words. Let your words invite a limitless mindset, not a limited mindset. What you speak aloud wires your mind to believe what you are saying, and you will embrace it to be a part of your spiritual foundation. My friend, the words that you speak are not powerless. Your words are very powerful. "The tongue has the power of life and death, and those who love it will eat its fruit" (Proverbs 18:21 NIV).

The prayers that you express to the Lord are a significant form of communication with Him. Therefore, you must let what you speak to the Lord through prayer coincide with what you speak aloud in your everyday life. You cannot pray to the Lord for a blessing and then let the words that you speak aloud make it known that you do not believe your blessing will ever come. The words that you communicate to God must rest in agreement with your trust in Him for you to be blessed. What you say about yourself should make your thoughts rise with power, not fall with doubt.

Speak positive things about yourself throughout the day. Begin your day with positive words about yourself. Continue your day with positive words about yourself. End your day with positive words about yourself. From speaking under your breath when there is a need for self-motivation to making a loud, bold declaration when the timing is right, let words of greatness come out of your mouth in a way that effectively fits you!

Let the words that come from your mouth give life to your faith. Let what you verbalize allow you to move forward, not backward. Let your words of faith overpower thoughts of failure. Prophesy a future of blessings in your life through your words. God listens to us, and He gives life to our words. By speaking blessings into existence, we open the door for us to see our instructions from God. When we speak greatness ahead of us, we embrace counseling from our Heavenly Father. "I will instruct you and teach you in the way you should go; I will counsel you with my loving eye on you" (Psalm 32:8 NIV).

One of the strongest adversaries to the optimistic words we verbalize are the risks that our blessings often require us to take. The words we speak tend to be best friends with the status quo, but intense enemies with risks. Nevertheless, no risk is too powerful for God. Do not be afraid to take a risk. You can regain what you have, even if you lose it. If you can do it once, you can do it again. If you can get a position at a company once, you can get it again. If you can become a business owner once, you can do it again. If you can purchase a car once, you can purchase one again. If you can buy a house once, you can buy one again. Let your words justify possibilities, not impossibilities. Keep in mind that a possibility stands strong as a reality when you have faith.

I remember a day when I was watching one of my favorite football teams in the last seconds of a game. Against all odds, the wide receiver made a difficult catch that put the team in field goal range. Shortly after, the kicker made the field goal, which was one of his longest-ever kicked. It looked as if they had won the game. However, the referee quickly made it known that the previous play of the wide receiver's catch was under further review. While waiting, the kicker could have verbalized words that he did not have the skills to make the kick again if he needed to make it. After all, it was one of the longest kicks that he ever made. Even so, he did not speak such negativity against himself. Moments later, the referee came onto the field and overturned the wide receiver's catch. Now, the kicker had to kick a field goal even further back from the far field spot where he previously made it. Nevertheless, he took his spot, kept the faith, and kicked the game-winning field goal.

Making the equivalent of a game-winning field goal kick in our lives is the type of thing that we must do, regardless of where we happen to be. When it looks as though our risks in life are too much, we must keep the faith. There is a reason why God has us taking risks in the first place. My friend, pray to the Lord for guidance about the risks that you will take in your life, and trust Him to lead and direct your steps. "Into Your hand I commit my spirit; You have redeemed me, O LORD God of truth" (Psalm 31:5 NKJV).

Though storms may rage in your life and attempt to cloud the eyes of your faith, continue to let the heart of your hope beat with confidence. Keep the eyes of your faith upon your blessings every day. Despite how things may appear on the surface, let the words of your mouth speak victory into your life. Speak your spiritual mind in agreement with the Lord! Speak greatness over yourself! Speak excellence over yourself! Speak blessings over yourself!

Times in life will exist when it appears as if the place where we are standing is too far back from reaching where we need to be. Even so, we must keep the faith! My friend, although you are standing at one place now does not mean that you cannot reach the place where you need to be at the time when you need to be there. Situations like these make me think about the coined term "Hail Mary," which was popularized in 1975 to describe Dallas Cowboys quarterback Roger Staubach's miracle-winning touchdown pass to his teammate, Drew Pearson. Sometimes you must throw a "Hail Mary" in life and keep the faith for the best to happen. If you are figuratively throwing a "Hail Mary," speak positive things to yourself about how you will be blessed, and keep the faith against all odds for God to bless you with His mercy. "I will be glad and rejoice in thy mercy: for thou hast considered my trouble; thou hast known my soul in adversities" (Psalm 31:7 KJV).

The words we speak work together with our faith when it comes to receiving our blessings. Think about the words that you speak when it comes to what you believe will happen as you are watching a television show. Why do you think what you are saying is about to happen will happen? What gives you the faith to speak such words aloud? It is because you have seen similar circumstances take place, so you feel that what took place then will also take place now. Be careful with this, however, because what you speak aloud is what you are expressing that you believe.

One of the most important things that we should do to make our words align with God's narrative for our lives is to read the Word of God. Too often we become frustrated with what is taking place, and we want to read God's narrative for our lives with our own words instead of the words that God has written for us. However, this is not how it works. When you pick up a book to read, do you read the words that the author has written, or do you read words that are not on the page, even though you want them to be there? This may seem like a ridiculous question, but it tends to be what we do at times when we read what God has written for us in the narrative that He has written for our lives. The best way to ensure that this does not take place is to familiarize ourselves with the Bible so that we will gain illumination and understanding of the Word of God that will carry over into our own lives.

A key reason why we want to read the pages of our lives in a way that we want them to unfold is so that there are no twists or turns that we do not want to happen. If things took place in our lives just the way we wanted at every moment we wanted, we would become monotonous readers when it comes to reading what God writes to make our lives. God makes us spiritually read each line on the pages of our lives with spiritual purpose and inflection. If things always worked out the way we wanted with no problem, then it would not take any amount of faith to make them happen, not even as small as a mustard seed. Knowing this, we must understand that God will not always make a perfect path for us to follow to gain our blessings.

There are times in life when we express the belief that we will reach a goal as long as one thing happens, and another thing does not. By doing this, we are placing limitations on ourselves. Have you ever been following directions to reach a destination, but you came to a change on the road that the directions did not tell you about? What did you do? Did you give up and turn around because you felt you did not have what it took to reach your destination because of the change? Or did you adapt to the situation, and do what it took to reach your destination? Instead of giving up altogether, it is more than likely that you found a new way to reach your destination. For you to enjoy a great outcome, your focus must be on the process, not merely the outcome. You must focus on the journey, not the destination.

While driving on the path of life, we must learn to adapt to things that we do not expect if we reach new points. There are many times in life when we want to pretend something is not present, but this often holds us back from moving forward. My friend, you must acknowledge something to move beyond it. If there is a reason you feel you need to see your doctor, then go see your doctor. If there is a reason you feel you need to check in with a family member, then check in with that family member. If there is a reason you feel you need to make a career change, then make that change. If there is an issue that you feel needs to be addressed with your significant other, then address it. Whatever is present in your life that you feel needs to be acknowledged, then acknowledge it. Spiritually provoke things that you know need to be provoked so that your faith will make you stand strong upon your spiritual foundation.

With a strong spiritual foundation upon which to stand, our eyes will open to see the strength that lives within us. Keep in mind that if no obstacles were ever present, there would be no need for us to have strength. Obstacles will come about again and again, but an obstacle is not something that will naturally stop you. You are not defined by the obstacles that present themselves in your life. The responses that you give to your obstacles are what define you. Your comeback to a setback shows the real you. My friend, there is no growth when there are no challenges. Presenting the strength within you that is driven by your faith in the face of a challenge pushes you forward, instead of holding you in the same place or pulling you back. Allowing faith to shine within your spirit gives you the drive that it takes to move beyond your challenges.

Never forget that those who surround you can often become a limitation in your life without you even realizing it. While there are some people who want the best for you, there are others who do not want you to rise above them. Although a person who has been in your life for a long period of time may seem to have your best interest at heart, this may change intensely when that same person realizes the blessings that await you. The same rings true for those who are just entering your life. It may seem as if another individual is someone who has no negative feelings toward you, but the exact opposite may be true without you even realizing it. Knowing this, you must hold strong to faith in all aspects of your life. Your faith will upset the insecurities of those who do not want to see you succeed, but it will make you rise above their actions to hold you back.

Someone who you know or someone who you barely know may both be attempting to bring you down. Do not let this take place. Pray to the Lord about those who are around you. Ask God to surround you with others who will lift you up, not bring you down. Even in the face of times when others have done things to limit you, do not let this close the door for you. Let your faith in God allow you to make negative things that others have tried to do serve as stepping stones that will lift you up.

Obstacles in life present themselves as other people, difficult situations, and even your very own state of mind. However, to overcome an obstacle, you must not allow any of these things to bring you down. Periods in life exist when obstacles win battles against us because we allow worry to overtake us. Perhaps you are sitting at home worrying about what you need to say to your boss tomorrow. Maybe you are worrying at this very moment about how you will pay a particular bill that is due. When all is said and done, what is worrying doing? ***Nothing.*** It is only wasting time that you cannot get back. Instead of allowing worry to be a strong point in your life, allow worshipping God to replace that as a strong point in your life. When you worship the Lord, He opens your mind to methods that will counteract obstacles instead of empowering them.

Worry and worship are not friends. Although we can spend a vast amount of our time doing one or the other, we cannot spend our time doing both. If you open your mind to doubtful thoughts, then worry will be what consumes you. On the other hand, if you open your mind to thoughts of praise, then worship will be what fulfills you. Have you ever heard someone sing songs of glory in a manner of worshipping God? Have you ever seen someone use their body to dance in praise of God to worship Him? Regardless of how you have observed someone worship God, each style of worship has one thing in common: ***It is a time when praise to the Lord rules that person's day.*** My friend, let your moments of worry become times of praise. "I will bless the LORD at all times: his praise shall continually be in my mouth" (Psalm 34:1 KJV).

Praise the Lord for your stumbles in the valley, as well as your rise to the mountaintop. Give praise to God when things seem right and when they seem wrong. Worship our Heavenly Father in the best of times and the worst of times. Praise the Lord as you look your difficulties in the eye, knowing that you will triumph on the mountaintop of greatness. My friend, always remember that the Lord will make a way out of no way. God will bless you to be a blessing to others.

Too often instead of praising God, we bring our complaints to God. We must remember that God does not work in a place of complaints. He works in a place of faith. God sees our faith when we praise Him instead of doubting Him. Our complaints stir up negative energy. This form of energy places a negative rift between the relationship that we have with God, which is certainly not what we need. Imagine if someone continuously spoke negative words to you, as you were planning to give them a gift. The positive feelings that you had toward them and what you were about to do for them would likely change to negativity. If someone was bringing an air of negativity to you, then you would likely give it right back to them.

On the other hand, if someone was bringing an air of positivity to you, then you would likely send that right back to them. Think about it like that with our Heavenly Father. As we send Him our worship and praise, blessings come our way. However, when complaints are what we send to God, we hinder ourselves from receiving our blessings. My friend, take your focus off your worries. Replace the time that you spend worrying about your problems with time that you spend worshipping our Heavenly Father.

Instead of allowing worry and doubt to guide your steps throughout the day, let your faith in God guide your steps throughout the day. Worry brings reluctance. Faith brings resolutions. Have the audacity within your spirit to face adversity with your faith. Remember that faith makes the trials and tribulations of today become the testimonies of tomorrow. When times get hard, combat the worry in your life with the worship of the Lord. Whatever gifts or talents that you have, use them to worship God. Do not make the mistake of worshipping your worries. Show God that you trust Him by allowing time that you could give to your worries to serve as time that you worship Him. Always remember that our God is a definite God, and He deserves definite praise. Worship Him through whatever means of praise you have. "From the rising of the sun unto the going down of the same the LORD's name is to be praised" (Psalm 113:3 KJV).

Sing praises to the Lord as you undergo your problematic circumstances. Pray to the Lord in your times of pain. Remember that your pain has a purpose, and communicating with God reminds you of this. Do not suffer in silence. Speak to the Lord through prayer and have confidence that no word will be in vain. Praise God before you receive your victory. Declare that victory will be the outcome of whatever it is that you are facing. Believe that you will overcome the challenges that stand before you. Celebrate the triumph of reaching your goals now, even though you are still pursuing them. With this combination, you will place yourself on the path to victory. "And if we know that he hears us in whatever we ask, we know that we have the requests that we have asked of him" (1 John 5:15 ESV).

Some people find it hard to celebrate triumphs in their lives before the triumphs come to pass due to the obstacles that currently exist. Do not let this be what takes place in your life. Embrace faith within your spirit so that you will step forward, not backward. Let your faith make each step you take place you closer to reaching your goals.

You will come across people in your life who may feel that the worries and doubts that you have are likely to come to pass. They may feel that worry has a more realistic place in your life than worship. Even so, never forget that God is the author of your life's narrative, other people are not. God knows your story better than anyone. Our Heavenly Father is who writes every page of our lives down to the very letter. Knowing this, your trust should reside in God instead of other people. Keep in mind that other individuals have their own lives to live. Just as you have issues of your own, they also have issues of their own. Always let your trust rest upon the Lord, not in your fellow man. Pray to the Lord and believe that He will bless you. "Lord, hear my voice. Let your ears be attentive to my cry for mercy" (Psalm 130:2 NIV).

Your walk through the valley is a time of spiritual enrichment. Some people only see the suffering that accompanies the steps taken while walking through the valley. Always remember that God has a reason for every season in our lives and a purpose for every happening in each season. God has a higher destination prepared for you. Trust that God will lead you through the valley.

One of the most difficult reasons why our steps are challenged as we walk through the valley is because of the connection that exists between two things in life: *suffering and success.*

A great relationship exists between suffering and success, yet this relationship is not one that tends to be clearly seen. My friend, keep in mind that despite what may be taking place now, there is a need to remain optimistic. Opportunities are born through optimism. The spiritual audacity that drives your beliefs is powered by faith. Your faith convinces you of your value. When you know that you are valuable, you know there is a reason to be optimistic. Have faith. Focus on the path that God has prepared for you. Fight for the best finish that being optimistic will bring. When this takes place, the suffering that you are experiencing in the present days will become the success that you will live out in the days ahead.

Optimism is an aspect of life that is empowered by the hope that we have for better times ahead. It hungers for desires of greatness to be achieved in our lives. Your optimism hungers! Your hope hungers! You must feed yourself with a connection to God so that you will rise into greatness! When you do not feed the hunger of your hope, negative things will feed it instead. Worry will feed your hope. Doubt will feed your hope. Pessimism will feed your hope. Things of this nature will feed your hope again and again until your hope becomes lifeless. My friend, let the hope that lives within you be fed by the Word of God. Let the hope that lives within you be fed by prayer. Let the hope that lives within you be fed by your praise to our Heavenly Father. Embrace a connection to the Lord and allow it to feed your hope.

Countless points in life often play out when we open the door for what has happened in the past to overpower our optimism. Times like these exist when we let our past mistakes take away the hope inside of us. Move beyond your past. Appreciate your present. Plan for your future. Do not lack the tenacity needed to rise when you fall. Paint persistence in your life through your trust in God. My friend, what has happened has already happened. Living in the past is simply walking in circles. By walking in circles, you are keeping yourself in the valley instead of progressing out of the valley. Let optimism be what you allow into your spirit. With optimism, we move forward. When we move forward, we reach the blessings that God has waiting for us.

Walking through the valley is a humbling time. It provides us with experiences that connect us with God, as we rise above the status quo. Life experiences are empowering to me as an author. I can see God's work in action through what takes place in my life, and it inspires me to be an inspiration to others. Whatever your life experiences happen to be, let your trust in God create a positive slant in your favor.

Too often I have seen how others will frequently worship the Lord when times are going well in their lives, but they will trade their worship for worry when times become hard. Worry and doubt will come together for these individuals, and faith quickly loses its place. Nevertheless, this is not how faith works when it comes to being blessed. We cannot have temporary faith for us to see God's power in action.

As well as not having temporary faith, we cannot have conditional faith for us to see God's power in action. Our God is the Lord of our lives every second of every hour of the day during every week of every year of our lives. We must wake up every morning trusting God and go to bed every night trusting God. When we trust God, our praise to Him overflows. Knowing this, we must keep in mind that God inhabits each and every praise that we give Him. "The LORD is my strength and my defense; he has become my salvation. He is my God, and I will praise him, my father's God, and I will exalt him" (Exodus 15:2 NIV).

Praise precedes your blessings. The praise that you give to God opens the door for you to receive your blessings. Pause with me for a moment. Imagine if God simply allowed your spiritual cup to run over with the blessings that He has prepared for you, and He required nothing from you. What would happen if there was not a valley to walk through before reaching the mountaintop? If that were the case, there would be no need for faith. We would not truly have to trust in God's power over our lives. What is wrong with that picture? Our Heavenly Father writes the narrative of our lives in a way that allows us to rise with faith, not remain at an entitled point of the status quo. Without a need for faith, we would not rise to greater places.

It may appear that life would be easier if you would simply stay where you are and not take the risk of a struggle toward success. Even so, what if you lost what is making you feel comfortable with remaining at the status quo? How would you bounce back from that? Would you still feel comfortable with settling for one point in life over another? Although it may appear to be the best thing for you to stay in your comfort zone, taking a risk is needed for you to rise to greater heights. Taking a risk brings about the need to have faith so that your blessings will come to fruition. Settling for what is ordinary may appear to be the easiest way to stay away from risks. However, being a child of God is not synonymous with being ordinary. If you were ordinary, God would not have extraordinary blessings in store for you as the outcomes of your risks.

A risk that you take today may set the stage for blessings ahead of you that generations to come will continue to be blessed from repeatedly. My friend, taking risks in life not only prepares you for blessings, but also enables the generations after you in your family to be blessed by your actions. Get out of survival mode and step out on faith to receive the blessings that will unfold from your risks! "A good person leaves an inheritance for their children's children, but a sinner's wealth is stored up for the righteous" (Proverbs 13:22 NIV).

Points in life when we take risks are often what lead us in our struggles toward success. One of the biggest reasons why we often turn away from risks tends to be the tests that go along with the risks. God will give you a test of faith not only to reveal your strengths but also to show your weaknesses to you. By making your weaknesses known, God will place before you what tends to hold you back from your blessings. As He brings this knowledge to you, God grants you the power to achieve heights in life that you never imagined. When all is said and done, there is one thing that you need to link you to the Lord as you pursue your blessings: *trust*.

Trust in the Lord blesses you to see the fruits of your labor. You must know where to apply yourself, and it cannot be against you. Apply your trust to God, not to the worries of your fears. Hold your head high with confidence that God will work things out in your favor, not low with doubt overtaking your thoughts. Your fellow man may tell you that your goals are impossible, but God specializes in making the impossible become reality. Do not worry about what you cannot do, but trust God regarding what He will do for you. Smile even when the raindrops of hard times fall upon you. Rejoice in the power of our Heavenly Father and let your trust in Him give you peace of mind on the best days and the worst days that you encounter. "Rejoice in the Lord always. I will say it again: Rejoice! Let your gentleness be evident to all. The Lord is near" (Philippians 4:4-5 NIV).

Wonder is one thing that comes about in our minds that should be a positive influence to us mentally, but it tends to have a negative influence instead. Too often we spend a significant amount of time wondering what will happen next on bad days, but not on good days. Time and time again, we wonder what will happen next only on the worst days of our lives. Nevertheless, if we would let this time of wonder unfold at a higher amount on the best days of our lives, we would give our lives the proper mapping that they need.

What is next? This is a powerful question that should not only have a place in your life on your worst days but also on your best days. You cannot just wonder what is next in the coming days when you are facing challenges. My friend, you must also wonder what is next when times are going well for you. It is as if you are finding one great puzzle piece to connect with another great puzzle piece so that you will keep the trend of greatness going in your life.

When we connect our thoughts of what is happening now with our thoughts of what is next, we open our eyes to see how we view the circumstances in our lives. By doing this, our spiritual vision gains clarity. With clarity in our spiritual vision, the path to our blessings becomes much easier to follow. You may need to be moved from one place to another because your spiritual vision may be limited where you are. The scope of your spiritual vision must be in line with the sequence of your blessings. As a result, God may need to move you from where you currently happen to be. When the vision of your spirit becomes clear, faith becomes what you use to look through life's circumstances.

With faith in your life, your momentary frustrations will pale in comparison to the great blessings that our Heavenly Father has prepared for you. Let your faith overpower your frustrations, as you trust that God will do His work in your life. Never forget that faith empowers you to expect your blessings. When you have faith, you do not march to mediocrity. You make bold steps toward your blessings. Faith makes a setback serve as a detour on your journey, not a dead end. Keep the faith that your tests today will become testimonies of God's greatness tomorrow.

Thank the Lord before you even receive your blessings, as you embrace the trust that He will show His favor to you. Remember that our Lord is three in one: ***God the Father, God the Son, and God the Holy Spirit***. As such, when we have faith, it is three-dimensional. Our three-dimensional faith serves our three-dimensional God. My friend, let your three-dimensional faith overcome your one-dimensional challenges! Instead of having anxieties when you encounter one-dimensional problems, trust your three-dimensional God! "Do not be anxious about anything, but in every situation, by prayer and petition, with thanksgiving, present your requests to God" (Philippians 4:6 NIV).

Chapter Six

MY VICTORY LAP

Win! *Dominate! Lead!* When faith is what motivates us, words that are synonymous with these words often steer our thoughts as we reflect upon the steps that we will take amid our exit from our walk through the valley. Regardless of how things may have been in your life up to this very moment, keep the faith! With this, your spiritual adrenaline rush will kick in so that your last steps in the valley will become the steps you will take in a victory lap, instead of steps in circles of uncertainty.

The way you think about the steps you are taking as you walk through the valley carries tremendous power. A high number of people have what it takes to move forward, but they cannot move forward due to the thoughts that they have of themselves. Capable people are often held back in life because of fear being the foundation of their spirit rather than faith. My friend, do not let this be you. Step away from what takes away your peace of mind, and step into what gives you peace of mind.

Time and time again, many individuals dwell upon being in the valley instead of ensuring they are taking steps that will allow them to move beyond the valley. My friend, it is not the valley that counts. It is your response to your time in the valley that counts. Each move you make as you walk through the valley is a response. Let every move you make serve as a bold response to your situation, not a moment of weakness. Allow your steps to demonstrate the greatness that resides within you. Hold your head high with trust that God will bless you to rise beyond the valley and into greater heights.

Before we even make one move, the way we think about our moves sets the stage for the time ahead of us in our lives. One word in reference to our moves stands alone with great power when we think of how we use it in our lives: **turn**. What is it about this word that carries so much power? Even without having the answer to this question, we still do our best to describe what kind of *turn* we want to take. There are countless times in life when we put forth the greatest effort that we have so that we may place one word in front of the word *turn* to describe the type of *turn* that we want to make: **right**. In this instance, a "right" turn parallels a "correct" turn.

A right turn is the type of turn that we become fixated upon making, regardless of what may be happening. In life, our focus often rests upon making right turns so much that the mere thought of making a wrong turn tends to be what has the power to deter us from pursuing goals that we are well capable of achieving. Always remember that no matter how things may appear, the direction that

God gives you is always the correct direction. Looking to the Lord lets you know where you are. When you know where you are, it helps you know where you are going. This is possible because your faith in God's guidance to steer your turns will lead you into better places.

When you have faith, what seems to the natural eye to be a wrong turn may bring about blessings that you never expected to occur or even imagined were possible. There are times when God will let a blessing fall upon you when you do not even expect it. A wrong turn may introduce you to a creative side of yourself that you never knew you had. Additionally, a wrong turn may lead you out of one field that you thought was the one for you, and into success in an entirely different field that you never thought about pursuing. Also, a wrong turn may allow you to meet your spouse, who happens to be the person you never would have met if you had not taken a wrong turn. My friend, do not always see a wrong turn as being "wrong." Look to God for guidance. Seek direction from our Heavenly Father.

Many people see a wrong turn in life as one of the worst things that could happen. However, God may be using that *wrong* turn to bring about a *right* turn. A wrong turn may be what makes you step away from what you normally do so that you will realize what you can do. Too often we want to emphasize the positive points in our lives and hide the negative points. Nevertheless, to reach higher places, you cannot only see what appears to be positive. When negative points present themselves before you, see them as learning experiences. You must learn from the negative so that you will grow.

By pairing what you have learned with the greatness that exists within you, significant growth will flourish in your life.

To reach points of growth, we must learn to overcome the obstacles in our lives. Obstacles that present themselves before a person are a key factor as to why well-qualified individuals tend to turn away from their goals. People often stop in their tracks when they meet resistance on the road of life. Many people would rather quit before making the effort to reach a goal instead of running the risk of making a mistake that would steer them away from reaching that goal. My friend, the mercy of God is greater than our mistakes! Never let the worry of a mistake stop you.

One of the best things that God uses our obstacles to teach us is how to spiritually gravitate toward strength during hard times. A time existed in my life when financial hardships served as the valley that I had to walk through. Only having a select amount of funds to put food on the table was a struggling point in my life, but I made up in my mind that I would take the necessary steps to move beyond this boundary. Although I had to take risks to reach my blessings, my faith during these times allowed me to be blessed. As a result, I gained the strength to overcome such financial challenges, and I used the knowledge granted to me to make me rise to greater heights in life.

A key lesson that this time in my life taught me was that I could take experiences from my own walk through the valley and make them serve as a blessing to others. On a random day while I was standing in line at a grocery store, a man in front of me did not have enough money to make his purchases. To help his situation, I voluntarily paid for his groceries. After this, I gave him my business card. I wanted to provide him with the chance to become knowledgeable about a business venture that I was a part of that greatly helped me financially. Within a few days, the gentleman joined my business venture. By training his skills, I made mine even better. This all started because I wanted to help someone who I saw needed something that I once needed. I knew that by being a blessing to someone else, I was sowing a seed for me to be blessed in the future. My friend, you can take your experiences from your walk through the valley and serve as a blessing to others, and have the blessings of the Lord continue to flow back to you. Being gracious to others brings God's grace back to you, and it encourages you to continually pursue God's grace.

Keep in mind that you cannot say in one breath that you have faith that you will be blessed by the outcome of your situation, and express that you fear the outcome of your situation in the next breath. You cannot fear your challenges and have faith that you will overcome your challenges at the same time. Faith and fear are mutually exclusive. You cannot have both at the same time. The two cannot dwell within your spirit at the same time. Just as a car cannot be driven on the road and parked in a parking lot at the same time, you cannot have faith that you will rise into blessings and have fear that you will fall into defeat at the same time. Spiritually gravitate to the Lord so that the faith within you will outweigh the fear that tries to weigh you down.

Days come about when we wonder why God would even allow low points to be placed in our lives if it is His will for us to be blessed to stand upon high points. Think of it this way. Why does it rain? Why is there sunshine during certain parts of the day, but darkness during other parts of the day? Why does the sun rise in one place, but set in another? Why are spring and summer two seasons of the year, but fall and winter the other two seasons? God uses points of darkness to bring about points of sunshine. He uses seasons of pain to bring about seasons of prosperity. Our Heavenly Father lets changes enter our lives so that we will enjoy better days ahead. My friend, the time that we spend in the valley is a time of growth. It is a humbling experience that prompts us to rise to greatness.

Although you are walking through the valley, God is with you. By the grace of God, you will finish your walk when the Lord leads you through your victory lap in the valley. His goodness and mercy are with you. No matter how challenging your situation may appear, always remember that the goodness of the Lord surrounds you. With each step that you take through the valley, be inspired by these words: *This too shall pass.*

As you walk through the valley, you learn to embrace the strength that resides within you. The time that you spend in the valley is a time of fruitful labor for your spirit. Although facing challenges may appear to be something that you wish would never occur, do not forget that God has a reason for your challenges. Walking into a challenge when a strong part of you does its best to convince you to walk away shows one of two things. It allows you to see whether you are ready to stand tall amid adversity, or if you will merely lie down when you are presented with pressure. Just as gardeners will wait until their flowers have flourished to pick them, God will wait until your time in the valley has allowed you to flourish to pick you out of the valley.

Each step you take as you walk through the valley is a time for your faith to flourish. By having faith, you allow your obstacles today to permit you to see positive outlooks for tomorrow. The obstacles that enter your life not only allow your faith to build, but they also give you a stronger sense of humility. There will be days when we walk through the valley that may seem like times when the only thing we can do is lie down in defeat. Even so, being at the lowest point of a valley teaches you to enjoy the privilege of standing on the highest point of a mountaintop.

The Word of God does not express that you must lie down in the face of hard times. It speaks of walking through the valley in which those hard times exist. Psalm 23 is one scripture of the Bible that stands out in my mind because this scripture makes it known that the valley of the shadow of death is not where we will dwell all the days of our lives. This scripture declares that we will walk through the valley, and it makes it known that we will not fear evil of any sort as we walk through the valley. "Yea, though I walk through the valley of the shadow of death, I will fear no evil: for thou art with me; thy rod and thy staff they comfort me" (Psalm 23:4 KJV).

Although you are walking through the valley with your own steps, never forget that the goodness and mercy of God are with you as you walk. The goodness and mercy of the Lord are with each of your steps everywhere you go. Our Heavenly Father does not say that He will "probably" have goodness and mercy go with you, or that He will "likely" have these spiritual aspects go with you. The Word of God expresses the bold, absolute word "surely" to make it known beyond the shadow of a doubt that goodness and mercy are with you, despite what happens to be taking place. "Surely goodness and mercy shall follow me all the days of my life: and I will dwell in the house of the LORD forever" (Psalm 23:6 KJV).

The fashion in which we take our steps as we walk through the valley often differs, but it serves the same purpose when done properly. Whether our steps are taken from a physical, emotional, or spiritual stance, we can take steps that allow us to make progress out of the valley. When faith lives within you and your trust resides in God, always remember that your steps are being ordered by God.

By making physical movements that are required for your progression, you allow yourself to physically step forward when you have faith. Imagine being confined to a wheelchair for months, but still regularly attend physical therapy classes, despite being told by many others that you should simply get used to being physically handicapped. Although it may seem as if there is nothing that could be done for you to recover, picture yourself standing up from the wheelchair without any help in front of the very people who told you that you would always be physically handicapped. This may serve as a happening that could inspire you to continue attending physical therapy classes, and eventually no longer be physically handicapped in any sense.

As you shed tears to express your emotions, you allow yourself to emotionally step forward when you have faith. By having faith as you encounter a challenge, you allow yourself to take an emotional step forward as you shed those tears, not backward. Days of depression may begin with you shedding tears due to being down about an issue in your life. Nevertheless, when you put your trust in God, you keep the faith that you will move beyond that issue. Resulting from this, you could become someone who later provides counseling to others after your tears of depression become tears of joy.

When you read the Word of God to spiritually connect with Him, you allow yourself to spiritually step forward when you have faith. Points in life may occur when you do not know how to embrace God in your life, but reading the Word of God will bless you to build a relationship with Him so that you will. Picture yourself surviving something that likely would never have been possible for you to live beyond. This may be what it takes to make you open your Bible and establish a relationship with our Heavenly Father. In doing so, you may then see the power of God in action so much that you reach out to others as an individual who spreads the Word of God to them. Regardless of what type of steps you are taking, those steps will bring you closer to completing your victory lap in the valley when you have faith.

One of the best things that we can do as we take our victory lap is to enjoy each step. Embrace the journey of your walk through the valley as you prepare to reach your destination. Close your eyes and envision this next point with me. Mentally picture a person on a track running the final lap that he or she will take before being able to step off the track as a winner. As this person takes his or her final steps, which of the following 2 thoughts in the mind of the runner do you believe would be more beneficial to have so that stepping off the track as a champion will be the outcome: *I cannot wait for this to be over!* **OR** *I can do this!* My friend, I cannot say enough about how important it is to keep a positive mindset about where you are instead of wasting your energy wishing time away.

Energy is too important to waste it wishing today's time away. In no way is wishing time away something that will help you. At this very second, you could be sitting where you are thinking about how much you want tomorrow to come because that is when you will be in the place where you believe it will be better for you to be. God may allow time to quickly progress to that future point to let you learn a very important lesson. The place you thought was best for you is far from where you should be. With this, you would learn to embrace places in time where you are without simply brushing them aside because you want a future time to come.

Instead of rushing time away, pray to the Lord for strength. Read the Word of God to gain a spiritual connection with Him. Set aside a time for meditation to boost your faith. Empower yourself as a true believer and follower of our Heavenly Father by surrounding yourself with others who have that same mentality. Make yourself thirsty for triumph, not compromising with defeat. Take constructive advice that you are given and allow the benefits of it to make you rise to greater heights.

What valley are you walking through? Financial difficulty? Health problems? Employment issues? Regardless of what you happen to be going through, let your faith in God's power keep you in the fight. As time passes during your walk through the valley, examine what God is trying to show you. Look at the imperfections that exist in your life. The imperfections in your life now can become points of perfection by means of our Heavenly Father's work. Despite any imperfections that you may have, God's perfection supersedes our imperfections.

No matter how your circumstances may seem, God's grace will bless you to make it through the race. God is not standing in the way of your goals. God is the way to achieving your goals. Have the spiritual audacity to confront any adversity that may stand in front of you. Take genuine steps. Take confident steps.

Commit to trusting God as you walk through the valley, as well as when you stand on the mountaintop. By trusting God, confidence is a strong point that will exist in your spirit. When you trust in Him, the Lord will bless you with the confidence that you need to boldly look any challenge in the eye that may present itself before you. When you trust God, assertiveness will also serve as a strong point in your spirit. Assertiveness and confidence are required to get where you need to be. Bowing down to your challenges gets you nowhere. Standing up to your challenges will take you anywhere. "Let us then approach God's throne of grace with confidence, so that we may receive mercy and find grace to help us in our time of need" (Hebrews 4:16 NIV).

Times have existed when I have seen people embrace a lack of confidence due to how they felt they would be viewed by others. "I would be great at this, but I did _______ in my past." "This is something that I would love to do, but if anyone finds out ______ about me, it would ruin everything." Reasons synonymous with these as to why people will not pursue things in life that they are more than capable of doing show me that instead of trusting in God, these people are trusting in other individuals. My friend, do not let the views of others make you give up on yourself. No one is perfect, but you are a masterpiece in God's eyes. Put your trust in God and turn away from your fears of the opinions of others.

Follow what God commands instead of what man demands. One second of following God's commands outshines a lifetime of following man's demands. It may seem as if it will be the best thing for you to go along with what another person demands of you today, but you need to step back and look at the situation. Is what another person wants you to do synonymous with God's desires? Let our Heavenly Father lead you, not your fellow man. If you see that what another person is directing you toward does not go along with what God is guiding you to do, then do not hesitate to choose to follow God.

By following God, we put our trust in His will. No matter how your set of circumstances may seem, trusting God is the key to bringing about better days ahead. You will have blessings unfold even when it seems impossible. Blessings in disguise will unfold as you walk through the valley. The days of your life will not always be high points. You must be able to step down to a low point before you can step up to a high point. My friend, never forget that the sufferings of your time in the valley are temporary, not permanent.

It takes strength within you to have faith in the best of times and the worst of times. God places certain days in our lives to show us the strength that we have, which we may not have been able to realize on other days. On days when setbacks storm into our lives, we have two options: *trust God or accept failure*. A setback is often God's way of turning us toward the proper steps we need to take so that we will have success. Always remember that God will supply all your needs. God will turn difficult times into advantageous points of excellence.

A problem that many people have when it comes to keeping faith rests upon one word: *silence*. Life tends to have seasons of silence as God is doing His work in our lives. Just as it is often awkward for us to sit in silence physically, we often feel awkward when we are in silence spiritually. Throughout the day, we physically hear noise in the background. Although we tend to drown out the noise, it is something that we are so accustomed to that it feels abnormal when we do not have it. From a spiritual standpoint, we want to hear God's work in our lives. When we do not, it can become so spiritually abnormal that it challenges our faith. However, silence will only last for a season, not a permanent length of time. God's silence does not bring suffering. It links you to the faith that it takes to reach your blessings.

A season of silence is a delay that serves as God's time for developing us. Although you do not hear what God is doing during this time, He is still working in your life. Think about when you are asked to stand for a moment of silence. This is a point in time that allows us to connect with God spiritually. Our minds become clear, and our souls invite God to come near. The next time that it seems as if silence is too much to bear, just remember that it is only a temporary season.

When it comes to you struggling in silence, that is an entirely different realm. The confusion that exists between the two tends to be why when we hear silence from God, we mistake this to be a point when He is not doing anything on our behalf. As you struggle in silence, the struggle still lives. This is why you must confront the challenge head-on that is causing you to struggle so that you will rise above your struggle. Practice positive actions that will grant you peace of mind instead of allowing your mind to be controlled by your challenges. Connect with God so that He will empower you to conquer your challenges.

One issue that exists when it comes to rising above a challenge is taking away its power over your mind. When you think about a problem, you empower the problem. A problem may exist in your life, and you have no idea how you will rise above it. What often takes place in such a situation is that you will wake up thinking about the problem, you will go throughout the day thinking about the problem, and you will even lie down thinking about the problem as you sleep. Look at all the time that you would happen to be thinking about this problem. This would serve as a significant challenge because you would be allowing the problem to overpower your thoughts with worry instead of allowing faith to overpower the problem. My friend, do not be tossed by the waves of worry. Let your mind rest upon knowing that faith turns the tide where worry has run amok.

Regardless of what type of problem may exist in your life, keep the faith with every step that you take. Faith makes you have a spring in your step, even when you cannot see the whole path that is in front of you. Let faith be your solution, not your alternative. Embrace faith within your spirit so that your mind will not be held down with worry, but instead be encouraged with optimism. Your thoughts and faith go hand in hand. You cannot have a weak mindset and see strong points of success come to pass in your future. My friend, your mindset steers your actions. What you think about either removes limitations from you, or places limitations on you.

No matter what problem exists in your life, always remember that you must turn it over to God. Imagine spending countless segments of time each day wondering why you are being passed over time and time again in your search for a job. Your problem of finding a job could be God's way of telling you to be your own boss. Our Heavenly Father could be preparing you to open a business that will be worth millions. When you take the time to turn away from your problem and turn to the Lord, there is no telling what you will learn.

Challenges often do something that we do not even realize is being done. They provide a new phase in our lives that will bless us to leap into greatness. There is a new song in your heart that you may not even realize is there, especially while you are confronting problems in your life. My friend, God places a new song in your heart for a reason. It is waiting to celebrate the victory over your problem, despite the natural eye illustrating to you that your problem is too big of a challenge to conquer.

Instead of taking time to think about your problems repeatedly, think about how you will sing a new song of praise to God after you have risen above your challenges. Do not give your problems power over your mind through worry. Let your faith open the door to your time of celebration in which you will stand tall on the mountaintop of triumph. "He put a new song in my mouth, a hymn of praise to our God. Many will see and fear the Lord and put their trust in him" (Psalm 40:3 NIV).

One key reason why God allows us to experience the challenges in our lives is so that we will gain knowledge. Being a knowledgeable person is one of the most powerful blessings that we may have. Whatever the knowledge happens to be that God gives you because of conquering your challenge, you must use it to have a triumphant foundation over the challenge that you overcame. The spiritual knowledge that God gives you must align with the actions that you take to see triumph in your life.

After we gain knowledge because of conquering a challenge, we then have a blueprint for how to go about handling future challenges in our lives. Whether it is a challenge along the same lines or one of an entirely different type, God will have given us a spiritual script to follow. Once you have been blessed to rise above the problems of yesterday, never think that God did not have a purpose for allowing the problems to be a part of your life.

Step back and think about how your life has changed for the better, and how your test may now be a testimony that will positively touch the lives of others. The tears you shed yesterday could be seeds that God planted so that your flourishing would not only have a positive effect upon you now, but also in the lives of others. After having your new testimony of God's greatness, your words may serve as seeds planted into the lives of others. You may be speaking to a total stranger in a coffee shop or standing in front of thousands of people delivering a speech, and what you have to say could turn the tide of someone's life in a positive way. My friend, rest assured that God has planted seeds of satisfaction that will flourish within you, and they will one day open the door to satisfaction in the lives of others. "They shall not be ashamed in the evil time: and in the days of famine they shall be satisfied" (Psalm 37:19 KJV).

Be a forward-thinking person, but do not overwhelm yourself with worries about tomorrow. There have been days in my life when I have confused being forward-thinking with worrying about tomorrow. During these times, I was not allowing today to set the stage for tomorrow. Instead, I was becoming consumed with worry about tomorrow. Nevertheless, I began to see that this was not a spiritually productive practice to exercise. It robs today of its needs, and it makes you unprepared for tomorrow. "Therefore, do not worry about tomorrow, for tomorrow will worry about itself. Each day has enough trouble of its own" (Matthew 6:34 NIV).

Take off the anchors of yesterday and rise into today. Whether you realize it or not, today has points of its own that are spreading the path for tomorrow. Do the best that you can with what you have today, so that you will be ready for tomorrow. Let today's happenings motivate you to spread your wings into tomorrow. Allowing anchors to weigh you down makes you a victim. Breaking yourself away from those anchors makes you a victor. By having the mindset of a victor, you will use what is taking place today to take steps in the right direction instead of the wrong direction. Concentrate on what is taking place today so that you will have a plan for how to be successful tomorrow. Let your thoughts see greatness ahead of you, not losses behind you.

The mind is a very powerful tool that significantly feeds the soul. Your thoughts can make you a prisoner of limitations, or a "prisoner" of God's work. Imagine thinking about your problems over and over throughout the day. With such a situation, you would be a prisoner of limitations. On the same token, imagine thinking about victory after victory to the extent that hope lives within you so much that your soul feels limitless. From this, you would boldly walk forward, not in a misled direction.

I once had the opportunity to meet a man who became a spiritual leader after sitting behind bars for years because of being wrongly convicted of a crime. Despite this, he remained a prisoner of hope instead of doubt, worry, or any other negative force upon his mind. Day in and day out, he would read the Bible, pray, and look to God for guidance. On a day he did not expect, he was informed that his case was being legally re-assessed. Soon after, evidence was brought forward showing that he did not commit the crime. He was then released. Having the mindset of a prisoner of hope instead of the mindset of a prisoner of so many negative forces that could have overridden his mind led him to keep the faith. Resulting from this, his situation turned from a test into a testimony that he shares with thousands upon thousands of people.

Whatever your situation happens to be, do not be a prisoner of it. My friend, do not be a prisoner of low self-esteem. Do not be a prisoner of depression. Let your "prison" be a strong fortress of the mind with hope so powerful that it makes your soul feel limitless, regardless of your life's situation. "Return to your fortress, you prisoners of hope; even now I announce that I will restore twice as much to you" (Zechariah 9:12 NIV).

Do not let your circumstances make you walk in circles. You do not want what is taking place around you to force you to stay in the status quo. In addition to this, do not let your circumstances make you walk backward. Wasting time and energy moving in the wrong direction is very problematic. Knowing the correct direction where you should walk is a powerful tool for you to have. Walk forward, my friend.

One of the biggest problems that makes us walk in the wrong direction is fear. Fear interrupts faith. It may be tempting to let fear make you compromise with what is beneath you, but that is not what is best for you. You cannot let the fear of falling hinder you from the opportunity of rising. The energy that it takes to have fear in hard times is the same energy that it takes to have faith in hard times. With fear, you live in spiritual poverty. With faith, you live in spiritual wealth. Embrace spiritual wealth and back away from spiritual poverty.

People often fear the likelihood that challenges will disrupt their lives. Although we may have what it takes to reach our goals, fear tends to make us vulnerable to the possibility that we do not. As a result, we become anxious when it comes to taking the necessary steps that are required to achieve our goals. Faith provides opportunities, but fear takes away opportunities. Fear makes us want to hold onto what is "normal," and push change away. However, you must have the spiritual audacity to challenge your normal days, so that you will reach better days ahead of you.

You must be able to deal with opposition to receive opportunities. With every opportunity comes a risk, no matter how small. Some people are so afraid of the slightest challenge coming about in their lives that they will stay away from risks that they are more than capable of conquering. Do not have that type of mentality. Let faith rest within your spirit, not fear. Be calm in chaos, not fearful of it. Look at challenges from a positive stance, not a negative stance.

Time and time again I have come across people who present themselves as being full of faith at church. However, you cannot have strong faith as you listen to the preacher on Sunday, but a lack of faith when you come up against your challenges on Monday. This is not an effective spiritual formula. The most effective spiritual formula is to let God be reflected as the greatest feature in your life, as faith shines through you. No matter what risk you must take or any challenge that you come up against, always remember that God is greater than anything that you may come across.

Times in life exist when what stops a person from reaching their full potential is the fear they have of another person. My friend, always remember that another person is still just that...*a person.* Although the individual may have a higher title, more money, or whatever the case happens to be, God is still on the throne, not that person. The power of God is not diluted by the actions of those who dislike you. Our Heavenly Father is not lessened by man. Nothing in life happens without God's approval. Instead of being fearful of your fellow man, trust God and His plan. "Fear of man will prove to be a snare, but whoever trusts in the Lord is kept safe" (Proverbs 29:25 NIV).

Pause with me for a moment. Close your eyes and reflect upon this question for the next 60 seconds: *Who or what in my life has made me give power to fear?* Open your eyes. Now, close your eyes and reflect upon this question for the next 60 seconds: *Why am I giving someone else or something else so much power over me?*

Open your eyes. What new findings has your time of reflection given you? Taking the time to think about who or what is holding us back in life is not something that we tend to do very often, but it is a powerful strategy. By spiritually evaluating our life experiences, we become able to see what is empowering us, and what is restricting us. God educates us through experiences. Our experiences are not meant to make us embrace fear over faith, but to let go of what limits us so that we will reach greater heights in life.

Too often in our lives, we allow unfounded questions that come to mind to prompt us to let doubt and worry gain control of our thoughts. Questions of this nature often stand between what we can do and what hinders us from doing it: *What will they think if I try, but fail? How will it look if I fail? Will I be able to face people who know me if I do not reach my goal?* My friend, when you consume yourself with thought after thought of the criticisms that may come from others if you are defeated by a challenge, you are giving others too much power over you. Do not do this. If these are people who you must wonder if they will think poorly of you if a door closes in one area of your life, then these are not people with whom you should surround yourself. Be careful who you let into your spiritual circle. Take caution about who you allow to give you advice.

Points in life may come about when people who feel there is not enough room at the top, so to speak, will do their best to ensure that others fail. These are individuals who will attempt to let their words and actions pull you down. Such individuals want to ensure that you succumb to the obstacles that challenge you from reaching your goals. Despite this, you must declare within yourself that you have what it takes to gain the blessings of God, no matter what others may think. My friend, make it known to yourself that you are a masterpiece of the Lord. Embrace the belief that God is who decides your destiny, not man. "For we are God's masterpiece. He has created us anew in Christ Jesus, so we can do the good things he planned for us long ago" (Ephesians 2:10 NLT).

Do not let naysayers intimidate you. Pessimists may be present who have nothing but negative words waiting for you. As a result, you may feel that the only way to avoid this is to make yourself look a certain way when you are around these people. Although it may seem as if having a particular person see you in a certain light would be a good thing for you, never forget that God is the author and finisher of your life, not man. Get in agreement with God, not with man. Take yourself away from those who do not have your best interest at heart.

If a person is not someone from whom you would freely take advice, do not let that be someone whose criticism you would freely take. Some people have criticism ready and waiting for you on a regular basis, but it is on a rare occasion that these same people have positive advice and compliments ready and waiting for you. These are not people who are working to help you move forward. They want to keep you from being the best that you can be. My friend, never forget that you are a fearfully and wonderfully made child of

God. Knowing this, do not let another person's criticism cripple your spirit. God has already ordained the right network of people to come into your life. Just keep the faith!

Some people only want to help you after you get where you are going. That is ridiculous! Do not take them seriously. Distance yourself from people of that nature. There are people out there who will jump at the chance to have you on a talk show, write an article about you, or offer to hire you as an employee after you already have a business of your own; and they now want to call you a friend when they did not care about you before your success. The funny thing is that these are often the very people who turned you down or looked away from you when you were trying to reach your destination. However, these people are now willing to help you when you do not need their help. My friend, you do not need directions after you have reached your destination. Remember those who were there for you as you walked through the valley and let those be the ones who you help once you reach your destination.

On a regular basis, time is often wasted thinking about those around you who do not have your best interest at heart. Although these people may have a great number of things to say about you, the things they have to say about you are against you instead of for you. Why would you give people who dislike you so much power over your thoughts? What makes you want to give them so much of your time? Do you think these same people who are against you would give you the same power over their time and state of mind? Please keep questions like these in mind the next time you begin to think about what such individuals would have to say about you. Although our Heavenly Father does not want you to have anger within you toward those who are against you, He still does not want you to give them power over your life. "But love your enemies, do good to them, and lend to them without expecting to get anything back. Then your reward will be great, and you will be children of the Most High, because he is kind to the ungrateful and wicked" (Luke 6:35 NIV).

Even a small amount of faith within you has the power to make you rise above the criticism of others, and triumph over the difficulties of your circumstances. You are not a victim of your circumstances; you are a victor of your circumstances. When you wake up in the morning, declare these words: *I am a victor!* As you go throughout the day, declare these words: *I am a victor!* As you prepare for bed at night, declare these words: *I am a victor!* Let this be a spiritual declaration that settles in your mind and guides your spirit so that you will stand tall against any set of circumstances that may come about in your life. Be a victor of greatness, not a victim of defeat.

Guidance is a point of significance when it comes to moving beyond the victory lap in the valley. You are blessed with guidance when the belief resides within you that you have what it takes to succeed. Even so, you must have faith for you to see your success before it takes place, so that it will properly unfold. Imagine talking to someone about a goal that you are pursuing, yet it seems as if all odds are against you. How would you explain why you are still pursuing your goal when it looks as if it will never come to pass? My friend, when you trust in the Lord, you have the belief that your blessing will come to pass. Your trust in the Lord empowers you to speak these words: *No matter how my situation looks, I will keep the faith!* Without saying another word, you would provide all the needed explanations as to why you stand tall against any challenge.

The steps you take as you walk through the valley are connected to your faith. What are you doing to demonstrate your faith? How are your actions showing that even though you do not physically see what will happen, you still believe that it will happen? Speaking to God through prayer makes you look forward to where God is leading you and away from where fear is trying to sway you. When you trust in God, you step forward with faith. My friend, keep a spirit of persistence within you as you walk through the valley.

Your walk through the valley keeps you from simply having a limited experience here and there. By empowering you with useful experiences, God builds your spiritual muscles. With strong spiritual muscles, you can lift your problems up and move them aside. Do not bury your problems. You must address your problems. When you simply bury your problems, you make them become bitter roots of your spirit. As a result, bitter spiritual fruit comes about in your life. Turn away from spiritual unhealthiness. An unhealthy spiritual side of you can produce an unhealthy physical side of you. Let health and wellness bloom in your life instead of having illness and pain hold you down.

We usually do not think about spiritual health, mental health, and physical health having a connection. Your spirit feeds your mind, which feeds your body. Think about times when you have eaten foods that should have allowed you to be fine physically, but it turned out not to be the case. How could that be? It is because what you were thinking about in such a situation wore your body down. Doubt and worry were serving as the mental foods that fed your body because fear overpowered faith within your spirit. In such a situation, this may negatively cause weight loss and lead to many health issues that a doctor may need to prescribe medication after medication to defeat. My friend, instead of allowing fear to bring about a broken spirit within you, let faith allow a merry heart to empower your spirit. "A merry heart doeth good like a medicine: but a broken spirit drieth the bones" (Proverbs 17:22 KJV).

By having spiritual strength within your soul, you have the power to take the steps you need to take throughout your victory lap in the valley. One of the most challenging parts of a victory lap is change. When we are used to something happening in a certain way, changing it to something different is not often what we want to happen. Imagine you have an appointment scheduled to take place, and you have been preparing to attend the appointment for quite some time. A change to this appointment may not be what you want to see. Canceling the appointment at one place so that you can go to another place would have a reason. God would be changing your location for a reason. As such, you would be in a different place than where you originally thought you would be for a purpose.

An unexpected combination that God brings into your life may change your perspective about a situation. Change is not always a bad thing, regardless of how you have been conditioned to view it. There are many times when a person has what it takes to advance in life, but making a change is necessary to see that advancement happen. With this, the person comes to a fork in the road: *take a risk to reach a new goal by making a change or accept the status quo to ensure there is no likelihood of failure.* Settling for less than you are worth can make you live beneath where you should be. There are times in life when we must take a risk by making a change so that we will see ourselves be the best that we are capable of being. Look to the Lord for wisdom when it comes to making changes in your life. Let Him order your steps into your blessings.

Even though differences take place in life when change comes about, there is one difference that we do not have to worry about: *Jesus Christ.* We do not have to question or wonder how Jesus will change, because nothing will be different about Him. The way that He was a part of the Holy Trinity yesterday is the same today, and it will be the same way tomorrow. No matter what difference may come about because of change, remember that Jesus is with you. Nothing about Him has changed, nothing about Him is changing, and nothing about Him will change. "Jesus Christ *is* the same yesterday, today, and forever" (Hebrews 13:8 NKJV).

Change is often the needed ingredient in the recipe for our goals to spiritually materialize. Remaining in the status quo tends to be a limiting factor in our lives, and it keeps us from crossing the finish line of the victory lap. Although the changes that take place in our lives may not be what we want to see, we must trust God's plan. We serve a strategic God. Although frustration may enter your life along with the changes that come, keep the faith. Let your trust reside in our Heavenly Father's plan for your life. Do not let your frustration hinder your faith. "For my thoughts are not your thoughts, neither are your ways my ways," declares the Lord. "As the heavens are higher than the earth, so are my ways higher than your ways and my thoughts than your thoughts" (Isaiah 55:8-9 NIV).

Detours in life may result from changes taking place. Even so, a detour does not bring an end to God's plan for you. A detour often arrives because God will not let you have something when He knows you are settling for it. He may have you walking through the valley so you will walk around a lower opportunity and reach a higher opportunity. Although a detour may delay the timing in which you expect your blessing, this does not mean that your blessing will not come. We often see detours in our lives as disappointments. My friend, disappointment in one place may be God's way of preparing you for an appointment in another place. Never forget that God is navigating your steps as you walk through the valley.

Experiencing changes in life may be spiritually painful. Nevertheless, the steps you take in pain as you walk through the valley have a purpose behind them. A time of pain will not stop your blessings from materializing. God has already ordained the very second of your blessings. While a change may appear to your natural eyes as a bad thing, look through your eyes of faith so that your confidence in God's plan for you will encourage you to trust Him. Do not let what appears to be a bad situation reroute your expectations. Expect to be blessed! Expect God's favor! "You will arise and have compassion on Zion, for it is time to show favor to her; the appointed time has come" (Psalm 102:13 NIV).

There are times in our lives when we will go through storms. When God allows rain into our lives, He is blessing us with growth. Imagine if there was sunshine all the time. While that seems as if it would be a good thing, picture something with me for a moment. Let your mind envision a flower planted in the soil. If nothing but sunlight was on this flower, day in and day out, the flower would dry up at some point. Now, picture points of time when rain interrupts the sunlight. This would not only keep the flower alive, but it would also allow the flower to blossom. Just as a change in physical weather needs to take place for a flower to see its best, a change in spiritual weather needs to take place for you to see your best.

Rough tides may move at certain times in your life, but keep in mind that the Lord leads us beside still waters. The same rough tides that will move uncontrollably at one moment will become still waters when God speaks for a time of peace to occur. When God speaks events into existence, His power is boldly shown. My friend, the same God who brought darkness during the daytime in the days of Moses is the same God who brought darkness at the height of day with the total solar eclipse during the 21st century. "Then the LORD said to Moses, "Stretch out your hand toward the sky so that darkness spreads over Egypt—darkness that can be felt" (Exodus 10:21 NIV).

The change in how the sky is normally demonstrated during daytime was a change that caught the attention of millions of people throughout the world, and it is a change that I saw with my own eyes. Having the total solar eclipse bring about 4 minutes of totality showed the natural eyes God's power in action. During the total solar eclipse, I recall floods of quietness among the individuals around me, because of them being stunned in silence. Being able to see such a miraculous happening in real time was a reminder of the power of God. "And it shall come to pass in that day," says the Lord GOD, "That I will make the sun go down at noon, And I will darken the earth in broad daylight" (Amos 8:9 NKJV).

Time and time again, the way a situation "looks" makes it appear to be unconquerable. My friend, the next time you encounter a challenge that seems to be too much for you to bear, just remember the power that God holds. Keep in mind that the same power that can bring a change so bold in the height of day that it gets the attention of millions of people is the same power that can bring a bold blessing in your life that is higher than any challenge. Even so, God may still use one thing that is necessary to bring about that blessing: *change.*

When changes occur in our lives, the status quo is interrupted. Life's interruptions are a key reason why we tend to make a great effort to stay away from change. Interruptions bring pauses to what we see as normal. Although a pause tends to occur with change, we must remember that God has already laid the path for us to follow once things resume. Worries of whether we will get back to the place where we were before the interruption usually flood our minds. Nevertheless, how could we get out of the valley if we were only to remain in the same place? It takes movement into a better place for your walk through the valley to only be temporary.

One of the best things for us to keep in mind about our walk through the valley is that it is only *temporary.* As we keep in mind that things that appear to be the worst points of our lives are only *temporary*, this empowers us to have faith during these challenges. Triumph begins with your thoughts. Optimistic thoughts are driven by your faith. By having faith live within you instead of doubt, you have power within yourself to accomplish great things. Take your worst and make it your best! The next time that the steps you take as you walk through the valley seem to be too much to handle, just remember that it is a time in your life that is only temporary. "So, we fix our eyes not on what is seen, but on what is unseen, since what is seen is temporary, but what is unseen is eternal" (2 Corinthians 4:18 NIV).

Your approach to your obstacles is often what sets the stage for how challenging they will be or will not be. Some people dive into a challenge without a second thought and without any size of faith. This sets them up for failure before the situation even begins. My friend, look to God for guidance and allow faith within your spirit to grant you peace of mind. Too often I have seen people back down from obstacles because of the belief that they do not have what it takes to become triumphant. Do not have this type of mentality. Just let these words echo inside of you: *God made me the way He made me for a reason!*

Always remember that you are a fearfully and wonderfully made child of God! God gave you life on purpose. He lets you live each day on purpose. Although you may not be the picture of perfection, you were made in the image of the Lord. Instead of looking aside to delay the inevitable, look up to God for inspiration. With this, you will look straight at your challenge with confidence that God will work the situation out in your favor. Do not doubt yourself. Do not just work to beat the odds. Defy the odds! Let confidence live within you! Let faith live within you! Remember that a fall in one place is an elevation in another place. Rest assured that God will shine a light on your darkest days, just as He does on your brightest days.

As God elevates you to higher places in life, one of the best lessons that you will learn is that the easiest path to follow is not always the best path to take. The desire to take each step that you will make with ease is at times one of the most combative things that may stand in front of you. When one path's approach does not entail a challenge, but another path does, thoughts like these tend to come to life: *This is a much easier way to do this. It is probably best that I do it this way so that I do not run the risk of failing.* Do not let doubt lead your mindset toward defeat before you even take one step. You are bound by the limitations that doubt brings, but you are released by faith. Doubt makes you pitiful, but faith makes you powerful. Always remember that although your journey includes a walk through the valley, it does not include a final rest there.

Transitioning from a time in the valley to stepping across the finish line of your victory lap in the valley requires an investment in yourself. Do not get up in the morning with no investment in yourself for the day. Do not go throughout the day with no investment in yourself. Do not lie down at night with no investment in yourself for the upcoming day. Whether it is an investment of your time, your thoughts, your actions, or whatever the investment happens to be, let it be something that makes you move forward.

Although the steps that you are taking in life may be in the valley at this time, you will walk with authority when your trust resides in the Lord. Our Heavenly Father takes you on a walk through the valley so that you will find balance in your life. By doing this, He strengthens your faith. As your faith gains strength, you gain balance as you walk through the valley. With strength within yourself, you take authority over your situations instead of allowing your situations to take authority over you. The valley you are walking through may seem so difficult with each step you are taking because God's plan for your life has greatness far beyond anything you ever expected to serve as the outcome of your steps beyond the valley. By having you walk through the valley, God teaches you to have hope in the midnight hour and appreciation of the brightest hour. Hold strong to the belief that your struggles are steering you toward success.

Someone living in a homeless shelter may have a job interview in the coming hours that could set the stage for a level of financial stability that may end homelessness in this person's life. With faith, the walk that this person is taking through financial struggles may end within a matter of hours after this job interview. Just like the person mentioned here, moving forward for you could certainly be a complication. However, a complication is not something that will stop you from reaching your destination when you have faith. No matter how strong the storm may seem, keep the faith! Let your trust in God be your song in the storm!

God would not have allowed you to take one step into the valley if He did not already have His hands around you for protection. The valley was created by the Lord. Every place you walk through has approval from Him, and every place has a purpose. Changes will take place in your life with the steps that you will take. The Lord will lead you from where you were to where He wants you to be. The point of your life when you step into the valley will be much different from the point of your life when you step out of the valley. Even so, God's protection is around you every morning when you wake up, every day you go about your life, and every night when you lie down to rest. "Even to your old age and gray hairs I am he, I am he who will sustain you. I have made you and I will carry you; I will sustain you and I will rescue you" (Isaiah 46:4 NIV).

Time and time again, defeat is the outcome that we allow to overpower our minds instead of letting a mindset of optimism do its work within us. Continue to remember that you are walking *through* the valley. It is *not* a permanent place for you. It is only temporary. When you declare within yourself that you are only in the valley for a temporary point of time, you are allowing a mindset of triumph to overpower a mindset of defeat. The valley may give you a taste of defeat, but God always blesses you with a full plate of victory as you smell triumph.

I cannot say enough that something in your life that may be holding you back is something that you are not allowing yourself to see is holding you back: *your fellow man*. Your fellow man may be one of the strongest things against your progression in life without you even realizing it. Although your fellow man may try to gain control of your mind by having you succumb to a negative view of your situation, do not release power over your mind to another person. Always keep in mind that faith will turn the pain of this very second into prosperity throughout the coming years when you trust in God. With faith, the pain that you feel at one moment leads you to promotion in the moments to come. The suffering that you have at one time sets you up for success ahead of you when faith resides within you. Faith is a weapon against frustration. Faith is a weapon against pain. Faith is a weapon against failure. Faith is a catalyst in the spiritual reaction of your situation that prompts blessings to occur. Knowing this, let the tears you cried yesterday water the seeds you plant today for the blessings that will blossom in your life tomorrow.

When you worry you do not wipe away today's problems, nor do you clear a path for a better tomorrow. You wipe away the peace of today, and you place tomorrow at a low starting point. Worry allows fear to dictate your spirit and control your mind. This is a pitfall that holds you down, and it keeps you from moving forward. On the other hand, when you trust God, you open the door to greatness beyond anything that you may have never imagined. "For God has not given us a spirit of fear, but of power and of love and of a sound mind" (2 Timothy 1:7 NKJV).

Remember that God is feeding your situation with His power. My friend, one crumb that falls from the table of the Lord is more filling than a meal from the table of man. When God feeds you, He will bless you to move beyond the valley and reign upon the mountains ahead of you. God will bless you to stand triumphantly at the mountaintop, regardless of what you must stand over. Not only is our Heavenly Father by your side when you are at the highest points of your life, He is also by your side when you are at the lowest points.

Just as time in the valley can starve your greatness at certain points, it can also feed your greatness at many other points. One of the main things that we must pay attention to for us to be fed and not starved is God's punctuation as He writes the pages of our lives. As we keep in mind that God is the author of our lives, we must pay attention to how He is writing our lives. Steps that we take in the valley may seem like times when God is placing a period, but they may be a times when He is placing a comma. What is the difference? A period brings about an ending, but a comma is simply a pause. God's gift to you of this type of knowledge feeds you so that you are well-prepared to successfully walk through the valley. Rejecting you from one area of life is often God's way of protecting you from following a lesser path so that you will reach greater heights. A time of rejection may place a comma in a sentence of your life so that the next part of the sentence will be a blessing far beyond your expectations.

Being in the valley allows you to learn the path that God wants you to follow. Once you find your way, it is much easier to maneuver in life. A particular night when I was traveling to a wedding with my mother demonstrated this to me very well. At the time, I was unsure how to reach the destination because I was in unfamiliar territory at night. However, when I saw a sign that gave me direction, this put me at ease. Soon after gaining the proper direction, we reached our destination. Knowing the direction of your path in life is one of the most important things when it comes to being blessed. Gaining direction in life is one of the strongest happenings that can take place for you.

As you walk through the valley on your victory lap, knowledge will be seen as one of the greatest gifts given to you. If something is not meant for you to know, then do not worry about it. On the other hand, if it is meant for you to know, keep the faith that God will bless you to know it. One of the best pieces of knowledge for you to learn is that God writes every line on each page of your walk through the valley because He is the author of life. Although walking through the valley may seem like one of the worst things that God could allow to happen in your life, it is in His plan for a reason.

Imagine receiving a letter of denial to a college that you had your heart set on attending. Picture being turned down for a mortgage loan for a home that you thought you would get. Times will exist in life when the things that you want to happen will not happen so that better things will happen. God may be using your walk through the valley as a time for you to see that what appeared to be your second choice is your best choice. With this, He will make your steps smooth on a different path as you walk through the valley.

Your time in the valley teaches you that you will either walk through the valley, or the valley will walk over you. Do not see your walk through the valley as a time when things happen to you. Let it be a time when you see things happening for you. Your walk through the valley is a time of testing. When you take your first step, it may seem as if there is no way that you could make it out of such a place. However, taking more steps will show you the greater strength that lives within your spirit. As you take steps to walk out of the valley, you will see the reality that even the darkest night has a new day ahead. To help this knowledge spiritually register within you, I have something to ask of you. The next day that you wake up, tell yourself these words: *It is a new day. It is a new time. It is a day for me to live anew.*

While you think of how difficult walking through the valley may seem to you, think about how Jesus Christ Himself had a valley of His own to walk through. His time physically on Earth was a time for Him to take steps in our shoes, as He opened the door to our salvation. Jesus had pain and suffering to endure for the benefit of humanity. Despite His challenging times, Jesus performed miracle after miracle instead of merely seeing the negative viewpoints of His valley. Jesus took His victory lap by rising from crucifixion to resurrection with all the power of Heaven and Earth in His hands. The next time things in life appear to be too much for you to handle, just remember the sacrifices that Jesus put forth for us to have salvation.

No matter what valley you happen to be walking through, always remember that the Lord is with you. If your valley is homelessness, God will bless you to walk out of it. If your valley is financial distress, God will bless you to walk out of it. If your valley is incarceration, God will bless you to walk out of it. If your valley is a point of life lying in a hospital bed as you fight an illness, God will bless you to walk out of it. Your steps in the valley are walked in the spirit, not in the flesh. As such, faith is what keeps your spirit strong so that you will walk out of the valley, not viewing your situation as it appears on the surface.

Walking through the valley may bring about feelings of worry, doubt, depression, and sadness. However, would the same things that are causing you to have such mental burdens be so important if you learned that you only have 5 minutes left to live? Most likely not. Your entire focus would likely shift. With that said, why give a short span of life more focus on important things than you would give them in a long lifespan? Why enjoy your life only if you have a small amount of time left to live instead of also enjoying your life when you are blessed with many years of life to come?

Regardless of what may be happening in your life, take the time to see what God is showing you in both good and bad times. Acknowledge the greatness that He has placed within you, and trust in His power. Know that every stumble is a point for you to spring forth to greater places than where you were before. Take authority over your steps in the valley instead of allowing your steps to make you fall. Remember that God will present you with what appear to be trivial things, but they will have effects so great that you may never have imagined such blessings. "That the communication of thy faith may become effectual by the acknowledging of every good thing which is in you in Christ Jesus" (Philemon 1:6 KJV).

Keep in mind that power and purpose come together as God writes the pages of your life. Picture taking on a second job so that you can pay your utility bills. However, in doing so, you may learn a new skill that will empower you to start a business that makes you financially prosper beyond anything that you could have ever imagined. Despite how your current situation may seem, remember that there is still something positive to take from it. Our Heavenly Father is writing the pages of your time in the valley the way that they happen to be for a reason. The steps you are taking have a purpose. He simply needs you to trust in Him and keep the faith. God is great every day, and God is great in every way! As a child of God, always remember that it is a great day for you to be great! My friend, peace be with you!

ABOUT THE AUTHOR

By unifying his passion for writing with his art of motivational speaking, Vempre Terrell, Jr. touches the lives of individuals with encouraging words, time and time again. He makes it known that hearing one simple word, reading a Bible scripture, or speaking with a person who needs someone to talk to often serves as an inspiration for him when it comes to writing.

Whether speaking to one person or one thousand people, Vempre loves to motivate others. Whether having one person read his books or one thousand people read his books, Vempre loves to motivate others. In the words of this fine gentleman: *Nothing is impossible when your faith rests upon the power of God.* **MY WALK THROUGH THE VALLEY** is Vempre Terrell, Jr.'s second published book; his first book is **THE EYES OF FAITH.**